D1288701

SECURING APPROVAL

CHICAGO SERIES
ON INTERNATIONAL &
DOMESTIC INSTITUTIONS

Edited by
William G. Howell and Jon Pevehouse

ALSO IN THE SERIES:

After the Rubicon: Congress, Presidents,
and the Politics of Waging War
by Douglas L. Kriner

=

SECURING APPROVAL

DOMESTIC POLITICS

AND MULTILATERAL

AUTHORIZATION FOR WAR

Terrence L. Chapman

THE UNIVERSITY OF CHICAGO PRESS

CHICAGO AND LONDON

TERRENCE L. CHAPMAN is assistant professor in the Department of Government at the University of Texas, Austin. He is the author or coauthor of several articles that have appeared in the *Journal of Politics*, *International Organization*, *International Studies Quarterly*, and the *Journal of Conflict Resolution*.

The University of Chicago Press, Chicago 60637
The University of Chicago Press, Ltd., London
© 2011 by The University of Chicago
All rights reserved. Published 2011.
Printed in the United States of America

20 19 18 17 16 15 14 13 12 11   1 2 3 4 5

ISBN-13: 978-0-226-10121-7 (cloth)
ISBN-13: 978-0-226-10122-4 (paper)
ISBN-10: 0-226-10121-5 (cloth)
ISBN-10: 0-226-10122-3 (paper)

Library of Congress Cataloging-in-Publication Data

Chapman, Terrence L.
    Securing approval : domestic politics and multilateral authorization for war / Terrence L. Chapman.
        p. cm.
    Includes bibliographical references and index.
    ISBN-13: 978-0-226-10121-7 (cloth : alk. paper)
    ISBN-13: 978-0-226-10122-4 (pbk. : alk. paper)
    ISBN-10: 0-226-10121-5 (cloth : alk. paper)
    ISBN-10: 0-226-10122-3 (pbk. : alk. paper) 1. War, Declaration of—Decision making. 2. International agencies. 3. United Nations. Security Council. 4. International agencies—Influence. 5. Military policy—Public opinion. 6. Security, International. 7. International relations. I. Title.
    JZ4850.C43 2011
    341.6'2—dc22

                                                                2010020387

♾ This paper meets the requirements of ANSI/NISO Z 39.48–1992 (Permanence of Paper).

CONTENTS

ILLUSTRATIONS

ACKNOWLEDGMENTS

I accumulated too many intellectual and personal debts during the writing of this book to hope to ever repay fully. Many colleagues and friends (including some who began as strangers but became friends throughout this process) offered advice and criticism that have helped make this book immeasurably better. I am extremely grateful for their help and do not think this book could have been completed without all the incredible feedback. I offer my sincerest apologies if I leave anyone out of the following acknowledgments. Of course, all errors are my own.

First, I would like to thank my mentors during my graduate training at Emory University: Cliff Carrubba, David Davis, Eric Reinhardt, and Dani Reiter. Each provided me with considerable attention and challenged me to think harder about asking good questions and constructing careful answers to those questions. I am very lucky and grateful to have had their mentorship early on in my scholarly career and I continue to benefit from their insights and advice. I owe a special debt to Dani Reiter for all of his time and help.

Second, I was fortunate to overlap in graduate school with a group of very talented international relations scholars and wonderful friends, many of whom provided useful suggestions both formally and in informal conversation. Those who read portions of this project or offered advice along the way include Zaryab Iqbal, Emily Hencken Ritter, Scott Wolford, and Amy

Yuen. Many others also helped build an energetic and positive environment for studying international relations.

I also owe a great deal to my colleagues at the University of Texas. Jason Brownlee, George Gavrilis, Stephen Jessee, Pat McDonald, Peter Trubowitz, Harrison Wagner, and Kurt Weyland all read either parts or the entire manuscript in its early stages and offered me unrelenting criticism. Stephen Jessee generously agreed to let me use portions of preliminary experimental results from a coauthored project in chapter 4. Pat McDonald and Harrison Wagner read multiple drafts of several sections, pushed me to think harder about how to communicate my ideas, and provided insight into academic publishing. Pat McDonald, Bat Sparrow, Peter Trubowitz, and Kurt Weyland gave important advice on crafting a prospectus and navigating the publishing process. Daron Shaw and Nick Valentino answered my questions about both publishing and the American political behavior literature. My department chair, Gary Freeman, provided considerable encouragement, advice, and research support throughout the process. A research fellowship and grant from the College of Liberal Arts also made this project possible. Austin Hart, Jonathan Lee, Daniel McCormack, and Stephanie Seidel Holmsten contributed very helpful research assistance.

Many colleagues in the discipline also gave important critiques, some of them taking time to comment on early versions of the manuscript or even earlier papers that were undoubtedly frustrating to read through. David Bearce, Jon Pevehouse, and Alex Thompson each read the entire manuscript and selflessly dedicated their valuable time to helping me improve the ideas and analysis. Other individuals that either commented on early versions of the argument in conference or draft paper form or offered suggestions in informal conversation include Julia Gray, J. Michael Grieg, Songying Fang, Mark Hallerberg, Michael Hiscox, Hyeran Jo, Ashley Leeds, Ken Schultz, Alex Weisiger, and Erik Voeten. Over the course of several years I presented portions of this research at Harvard University, Princeton University, the University of Colorado, the University of Maryland, the University of Pennsylvania, the University of Pittsburgh, the University of Rochester, and the University of Texas, and benefitted from questions and criticisms at each. A fellowship from the Niehaus Center for Globalization and Governance in 2009–2010 allowed me to complete this manuscript without too much distraction. Thanks to Helen Milner for the opportunity.

An early version of the arguments in chapter 2 appeared in the February 2007 issue of the *Journal of Conflict Resolution* and portions of chapter 4 appeared in the fall 2009 issue of *International Organization*. I thank both outlets for permission to use the materials and ideas in this book. I would also like to thank David Pervin, my editor at the University of Chicago Press, who provided insightful criticism and suggestions as well as wise advice. Mary Gehl did a tremendous job copyediting the manuscript. Two anonymous reviewers also offered important suggestions.

Finally, I owe a tremendous amount to my family, who encouraged me and gave me perspective through this long process. My mother, Margaret Chapman, has given me love and support and has reminded me to keep pushing forward despite temporary frustrations. My father, Edgar Chapman, helped instill in me a love for ideas. Both parents have offered me wisdom about academic pursuits. My brother, Ben Chapman, has always helped me get perspective on academic work and life. Spencer and Graham Chapman kept me company through many lonely hours of writing. Finally, my wife, Kathy-Ann Moe, has kept me grounded, taken care of me when I forget to do it myself, and offered unwavering support and confidence no matter how frustrated or despondent I get when trying to figure things out and write them down on paper. This book is dedicated to her.

INTRODUCTION

The recent controversy over the onset of the 2003 Iraq War raised important questions about the continued relevancy of the United Nations in world affairs. President George W. Bush posed the issue directly in his September 2002 speech at the United Nations General Assembly, asking, "Are Security Council resolutions to be honored and enforced, or cast aside without consequence? Will the United Nations serve the purpose of its founding, or will it be irrelevant?" In stating the issue in these terms, the president made the case that the relevance of multilateral security organizations in the twenty-first century depends first and foremost on their ability and will to enforce their decisions. Internally, however, administration officials were quite split over the decision to seek multilateral authorization. Secretary of State Colin Powell argued for working through the UN Security Council (UNSC) while others, such as Vice President Dick Cheney, argued against making external approval a prerequisite for military action. Although Powell's arguments about the importance of seeking approval eventually won out, the administration ultimately circumvented the UN Security Council because of the threatened opposition of several veto-wielding member states, France, China, and Russia, and several traditional allies, including Germany, and went to war with no formal resolution authorizing invasion of Iraq.[1]

---

1. Some argued that resolution 1441, passed in November 2002, was sufficient authorization for the war. See Wedgewood 2003 for discussion.

The administration's ultimate decision to proceed with the war despite the absence of a definite Security Council resolution authorizing the use of force appeared to be a defiant statement of its position with regard to the legitimacy or importance of multilateral bodies like the UN. But the question remains, if the United States (and by extension, other countries in similar circumstances) is under no obligation to gain the imprimatur of a multilateral body before deploying armed forces, why did the administration invest so much time and political capital trying to secure external approval? If critics of international law and institutions are correct and power is the ultimate arbiter of foreign policy behavior, why was so much effort exerted to curry favor with an institution that was publicly derided as politically unimportant or anti-U.S.?

The Bush administration's behavior is, in fact, not particularly aberrant. Rather, it is indicative of what is a relatively new trend in the international system: since 1945, political leaders have increasingly sought external approval from international organizations when conducting foreign policy. For instance, a similar dynamic to the pre-2003 Iraq War diplomatic effort occurred prior to the 1991 Gulf War, when President George H. W. Bush sought UN approval prior to military action. That administration succeeded in winning approval in this case, and public support for the war increased in the aftermath of the November 1990 resolution. The successful diplomatic effort at the UN in the summer and fall of 1990 likely resulted in the cooperation of key allies in and out of the region as well. The administration made a point of publicizing this activity, even creating a special committee on public relations that, among other tasks, communicated the international organization's support to the media and citizens at home and abroad.

Other U.S. presidents have also sought the approval of international organizations prior to undertaking military actions. President Bill Clinton garnered UN Security Council approval for the 1994 Haiti operation to reinstall the democratically elected and ousted Jean-Bertrand Aristide, and later sought NATO approval for the 1999 Kosovo campaign.[2] During the cold war the United States and its allies garnered UN support for the Korean War, which was called by administration officials "a considerable victory for Harry Truman" (Wainstock 1999, 23). Despite opposing superpowers holding vetoes during the cold war, the United States consulted or appealed to the UN in several important cases, including the crisis over the seizure

---

2. In the latter case NATO was preferred to the UN Security Council out of anticipation of Russian opposition.

of the USS *Pueblo* in 1968, the Cuban Missile Crisis in 1963, and following Iran's 1979 seizure of the U.S. embassy in Tehran. Even when intervening in its own backyard, the United States has sometimes sought some form of support from international organizations (IOs), as it did with the Organization of Eastern Caribbean States (OECS) prior to the invasion of Grenada in 1984. Remarkably, even during the early hours after the infamous Gulf of Tonkin episode, "administration officials . . . drew up arguments to be presented to the United Nations" (Karnow 1983, 387). The United States did not ultimately seek UN approval for the Vietnam War, but nonetheless administration officials seriously considered the possibility of pursuing multilateral approval for intervention in Southeast Asia.[3]

Attempting to garner multilateral authorization for foreign policies is also not a phenomenon unique to the United States. Leaders of other countries have often behaved as if winning some form of multilateral approval is important, if not vital, to military deployments. Tony Blair argued strongly for obtaining explicit United Nations backing for the 2003 Iraq War on the grounds that the British public would not support a war otherwise.[4] Other countries, such as Canada or Australia, make UN Security Council authorization a virtual prerequisite for participation in military actions (Voeten 2005). Even nondemocratic countries have occasionally brought issues to the Security Council, such as Egypt during the 1951 Suez Canal incident, Libya during clashes with Egypt in 1977, and the Argentine military junta sought support from the Organization of American States (OAS) during the 1982 Falklands crisis. Nondemocratic countries make these appeals less frequently, but when they do consult multilateral security organizations they use much of the same justifications as do democratic states. Clearly, external authorization has become a highly valued and sought after resource for governments. Recent scholars have gone so far as to claim that "foreign intervention without some effort to gain [external] approval is now virtually obsolete" (Thompson 2006, 2) and have noted that even powerful "states, *including* the United States, have shown willingness to incur significant costs in terms of time, policy compromise, and side payments simply to obtain the stamp of approval from the United Nations Security Council" (Voeten 2005, 528 emphasis added), despite the fact that approval-granting organizations lack strong enforcement power.

---

3. Notably, Robert McNamara, former secretary of defense during the Vietnam War, laments the lack of multilateral support in the documentary *The Fog of War*.
4. Woodward 2004 provides a good discussion of the role of Britain and Blair in U.S. decision making regarding the UN.

This book is therefore motivated by a central question: why do political leaders seek external approval from international organizations that lack direct enforcement power? Existing work has yet to understand both the policy motivations of these repeated efforts to secure approval, and the consequences of external approval and disapproval for the ability of leaders to conduct successful foreign policy. In fact, until recently, scholars have paid little attention to multilateral security institutions like the UN Security Council or other regional organizations whose primary function appears to be one of legitimization.[5]

Questions about the legal necessity of obtaining UN or other approval often arise in discussions about external authorization. Advocates of strong multilateralism sometimes suggest that authorization is required in order for an international operation to be legal.[6] But it is far from clear that leaders are legally obligated to seek external approval for their foreign policies.[7] For instance, commenting in 2003 on the legal status of Security Council authorization for the use of force, Michael Glennon writes:

> Since 1945, so many states have used armed force on so many occasions, in flagrant violation of the charter, that the regime can only be said to have collapsed . . . Given that the UN's is a voluntary system that depends for compliance on state consent, this short-sightedness proved fatal . . . Massive violation of a treaty by numerous states over a prolonged period can be seen as casting that treaty into desuetude . . . the violations can also be regarded as subsequent custom that creates new law, supplanting old treaty norms and permitting conduct that was once a violation. Finally, contrary state practice can also be considered to have created a non liquet, to have thrown the law into a state of confusion such that legal rules are no longer clear and no authoritative answer is possible." (2003, 18)

---

5. Scholarly interest in the UN was quite intense during its first twenty years of existence. A cursory glance at the pages of the journal *International Organization* from 1946 to 1970 shows considerable interest in the role and functioning of these institutions (e.g., Goodrich 1947, 1965; Claude 1966, 1969; Havilend 1965; Slater 1969). However, this interest seemed to wane throughout much of the cold war period, perhaps due to deadlock in the Security Council or the prominence of state-centric approaches to international relations theory. Since the end of the cold war and especially since 2001, however, renewed scholarly interest has resulted in work examining the politics and effectiveness of the UN (e.g., Voeten 2001, 2005; Thompson 2006, 2009; Coleman 2007; Hurd 2007).

6. See discussion in Rubin 2003, for instance.

7. Roberts 2004 and Glennon 2001 provide good discussions of the legal status of UN Security Council sanction. Of course, states may comply with international law out of reputational concerns or issue linkage (see Guzman 2008).

Other scholars note that since international law is fundamentally based on consent, compliance with or observance of the legal letter of law depends on the strategic interests or attitudes and beliefs of governments and statesmen, implying that legal obligation arguments are somewhat limited in their ability to explain patterns of approval seeking.[8]

Existing social science explanations offer only modest guidance as to why countries value multilateral approval. The traditional realist school in international relations tends to dismiss the role of international institutions, seeing them as mere manifestations of the preferences of powerful states.[9] This view is very compelling given that powerful states, like the United States, which sometimes eschew institutional authorization, are typically not directly punished by the institution or member states for failures of compliance or for acts of aggression. Sometimes smaller states feel the wrath of the collective members of a multilateral institution, as did Iraq after invading Kuwait in 1990. In such cases, however, enforcement depends on the willingness of powerful members to come to the aid of a fellow country, which is often unlikely when aggressors are large, powerful actors. The fate of large states that ignore institutional edicts is often tempered by the ability of others to punish without forgoing benefits those large states provide in terms of trade and stability of the international system (Brooks and Wohlforth 2005). The traditional realist perspective thus views institutions as only as good as their enforcement mechanisms, and for institutions like the UN, those mechanisms do not exist beyond the efforts of powerful members.

An alternative view is that seeking authorization is important for creating the perception of legitimate foreign policy. This view suggests that the public believes either that it is important to consult other members of the "community" before taking action, either as a matter of procedure or for the actual stamp of approval.[10] The latter belief—that an affirmative decision is key to establishing legitimacy—also implies that opposition can deliver a serious blow to international legitimacy. This view has considerable merit, inasmuch as in most of these cases cited above, leaders have either noted the importance of authorization for public support at home and abroad or

8. See discussions in Arend and Beck 1993, Franck 1990, and Glennon 2003.
9. See Mearsheimer 1995. This view is similar to Glennon's (2001, 2003), in that power politics is seen to play a predominant role.
10. See Hurd 1999, 2007. Voeten 2005 and Thompson 2006 offer rationalist perspectives on legitimacy-seeking. The distinction between *procedural* legitimacy and legitimacy conferred by authorization is important, as a purely procedural view suggests that the benefit of legitimacy may come from simply consulting an IO, regardless of whether authorization is actually conferred.

behaved *as if* authorization was intended to boost public and international support by, for instance, making public statements intended to justify seeking authorization. Indeed, in a famous article written early on in the life of the UN, Inis Claude argued that legitimization of the use of force through discursive means is perhaps the central function of the UN Security Council (Claude 1966).

Yet two puzzles remain that the legitimacy account cannot answer. First, leaders do not always seek authorization. Rather, patterns of behavior suggest that leaders strategically choose when to seek multilateral approval. For instance, leaders only consulted international organizations in roughly one quarter to one third of all international crises since 1945, as defined by the International Crisis Behavior Project (Brecher and Wilkenfeld 2000).[11] Of the actor-level observations in this data, which count one observation for each state involved in a crisis, the Security Council was consulted only 13 percent of the time, and regional organizations were consulted only 5 percent of the time. While keeping in mind that crises vary in seriousness, such that minor crises may not provoke approval seeking, the limited number of consultations suggests at least that leaders choose between several potential strategies to justify their foreign policies. Leaders seem to either know that sometimes seeking approval will not provide much of a benefit compared to the costs of diplomacy and delay, or if they believe that seeking approval would provide a benefit, approval from a credible source is not likely to be forthcoming, and therefore unilateral action or action with an ad hoc coalition is preferred. In either case, governments clearly make strategic decisions about the consequences of diplomatic efforts through multilateral institutions, which suggests that the legitimization account may be more complicated than is often depicted.

Second, authorization from a multilateral body does not always boost public support for military action, and opposition—or the decision to circumvent multilateral institutions—does not always diminish public support for action. For instance, failure to obtain a clear authorization for the 2003 Iraq War did not seem to decrease initial public support for the war in the United States. In other cases, such as NATO involvement in the Kosovo operation and OECS involvement in the Grenada invasion, authorization did little to increase public support in the United States. Existing studies provide little insight into the varying effects of multilateral authorization and opposition.

---

11. The actual percentage depends on how one treats consultations. In the following empirical chapters I discuss coding considerations in more detail.

This book provides an answer to why leaders frequently seek international organization approval, but why it only sometimes seems to alter public opinion. International organization approval can, under certain circumstances, provide valuable information to domestic and foreign audiences. In particular, approval can serve as a signal that a foreign policy proposal will not be exceedingly costly or overly aggressive. Opposition can also sometimes serve as a signal that a foreign policy proposal may have negative consequences. The problem is that, as with nearly all political institutions, decisions to grant approval for foreign policy are made by foreign governments, all with multiple and often competing interests when it comes to foreign affairs. Member states may have complex motives for their voting decisions, and those decisions culminate in the publically observable "output" of the organization: approval or opposition. Because citizens may be skeptical about the motivations of member states or may have only vague information about these motivations, it is often quite difficult for citizens to make sense of the signals emanating from multilateral institutions. The following pages show that, despite this obstacle, under many conditions the decisions of multilateral organizations can be quite influential for public attitudes, and this helps shape the strategic decision of governments to seek approval or circumvent institutional channels.

Information about foreign policy is important to the public because citizens ultimately pay most of the costs for military conflict, yet the average citizen does not have the expertise or information available to make sophisticated judgments about foreign policy. Citizens instead look to a number of sources for reassurance about their government's proposed actions, including opposition parties, the media, and the reaction of the international community. But when processing information, citizens often "consider the source." Not all sources of information are equally credible or trustworthy, as some sources have vested interests in the policies under consideration. We observe this fact in modern life when American citizens choose which media outlets to watch or which party officials to listen to. Citizens often must incorporate the perceived bias of particular sources when evaluating the informational content of messages (cf. Lupia and McCubbins 1998). These biases may in turn determine how influential messages are in changing attitudes or aggregate support for particular policies.

This book argues that citizens can similarly incorporate perceived political biases of member states when receiving information from multilateral organizations. Member states of these organizations frequently have a stake in foreign policy issues under consideration because the outcome of those policies often affects the distribution of power and influence in the international system. Thus, the degree to which citizens trust or learn from IO decisions is conditional on their perception of the political interests of IO member states. When approval comes from an unlikely source, in the sense that the voting members of an organization are unlikely to authorize a particular proposal unless it is not expected to be exceedingly costly or disruptive to international stability, citizens will tend to take this as a strong signal of the appropriateness of action. Since the organization is predisposed to only support policy proposals that are not expected to be overly aggressive and/or costly, the signal of support can help convince audiences that the policy is one they would like to support. However, when opposition comes from the same source, which was *ex ante* unlikely to grant approval, citizens receive little useful information about the expected costs of foreign policies. Since the organization is expected to oppose a wide range of policies, possibly good and bad, opposition does not tell audiences much about the potential consequences of a proposed policy. In general, this line of argument implies that under some conditions citizens react strongly to the decisions of IOs, in the sense that their support for their leaders and their leaders' policies increases dramatically, while in others citizens ignore these decisions.

Consider the case of French opposition to the use of force prior to the 2003 Iraq War. The position of France as a veto player on the United Nations Security Council prevented the United States from obtaining a second resolution authorizing the use of force to impose regime change in Iraq. From the perspective of the American public, two possible explanations may have accounted for French opposition. On the one hand, opposition could have indicated that the costs of invading Iraq were prohibitively high, relative to the costs of alternative strategies, such as continued monitoring and inspection efforts. The French government, having more access to intelligence and more expertise in foreign policy matters than the average citizen, may have decided that the benefits of invasion simply did not offset the costs. On the other hand, French opposition could have been the result of domestic political pressures, perhaps due to French business ties to Iraq, antiwar French public opinion, or French resistance to U.S. dominance. If the former were believed, the public would perceive the opposition of France, a vetoing member of the Security Council, as an indication that war would be prohibitively costly and would correspondingly alter the degree to which they supported military intervention. If the latter were believed to be the case, the inability to obtain a second resolution would not likely alter the decision of whether or not to support war, as opposition would be perceived as signaling more about

French politics than about the merits of the proposed foreign policy. The two possibilities have very different implications for the ability of institutions to constrain foreign policy. In the former case the Security Council could have a substantial impact on foreign policy behavior through domestic public opinion, but in the latter case the Security Council would be ineffective.

This general argument builds on economic theories of information transmission, which have investigated the conditions under which a receiver can learn from a sender who has private information.[12] Importantly, the degree to which information transmission can take place depends on the sender's incentives, which are shaped by the sender's preferences over outcomes. When a sender cares only about seeing an optimal outcome, or when the sender's preferences perfectly match the receiver, information transmission is easily achieved. However, when this is not possible, the degree of bias—meaning the degree to which the sender prefers one outcome to another—may provide the receiver with leverage with which to make inferences about the sender's private information. This logic has been applied to several political contexts, including the value of having biased policy advisors domestically or biased mediators in international disputes.[13] For the purposes of this book, this logic means that the degree to which citizens find the statements of IOs credible or useful in communicating information about the costliness of foreign policies, and in turn whether or not government leaders view securing approval as valuable, depends on citizens' perceptions of member states' interests and biases.

The arguments and evidence in the following pages have important implications for determining when and why leaders seek external approval, which might involve policy moderation or compromise. A common assumption in political economy scholarship is that leaders want to remain in office and avoid actions that have electoral or popular costs. This should be especially true for leaders in countries with domestic institutions that provide some sort of regular means of removal or political censure. In turn, leaders often may often try to exploit external approval and take pains to publicize it to their citizens, because such approval can lower costs of foreign policy for those leaders. This book examines this argument and its multiple implications for public reaction to IO decisions, coalition building, and the decisions of governments to seek external approval.

---

12. See Crawford and Sobel 1982; Farrell and Rabin 1996; Farrell and Gibbons 1989; Farrell 1995; and Austen-Smith and Banks 2000.
13. Calvert 1985; Kydd 2003.

RELEVANT INTERNATIONAL ORGANIZATIONS

What types of organizations might provide relevant information the public about the likely costs and merits of their leaders' policies? Multilateral security IOs vary in two important ways: membership rules and voting procedures. These are relatively durable features of organizational design that determine whose preferences are most important for driving decisions, and, in turn, the general approval-granting character or predisposition of the organization. In other words, these features determine whether an organization is most likely to be perceived as neutral, altruistic, or biased. Table 0.1 displays a list of existing prominent global and regional forums for security issues, along with their membership criteria and voting rules for international security issues. Beside the UN Security Council, which is the organization most frequently consulted by governments involved in interstate crises, a number of regional organizations act as forums for debate amongst members. The organizational "output" of these IOs are formal resolutions and decisions, or less formal but still public and official statements. Importantly, this output depends *directly* on member states' preferences. This differs from some institutions, such as the WTO, in which the relevant preferences for institutional decisions are those of technocrats staffing the bureaucracy or experts on dispute settlement panels.[14]

Each of these organizations contains in its charter provisions for the settlement of international disputes. Of course, the list of institutions given in the table is not the complete set of all IOs that have ever existed involving some collective security features. The list of all such IOs goes back at least to the Concert of Europe, a lose configuration of European great powers that emerged in 1814–1815 from the Congress of Vienna following the Napoleonic Wars. The Concert was not strongly institutionalized and eventually dissolved by 1848. A more formal attempt at collective security, the League of Nations, emerged from the aftermath of World War I. President Woodrow Wilson was a principal champion of the League, but despite Wilson's leadership, the United States never ratified the League charter. The League enjoyed some minor successes during the 1930s, but eventually collapsed due to its failure to answer Italian, German, and Japanese aggression during the 1930s.

---

14. Of course, some organizations, such as the International Monetary Fund, make voting proportional to monetary contribution, which raises the possibility of member preferences driving outcomes (see Thacker 1999; Stone 2004; Oatley and Yackee 2004).

TABLE 0.1   Global and regional organization membership and voting rules

ORGANIZATION	MEMBERSHIP	VOTING PROCEDURE
UN Security Council	Restricted by power status and regional representation	Unanimity among permanent five members, supermajority in total
UN General Assembly	Global	Majority or supermajority (depending on type of vote)
NATO North Atlantic Council	Regionally restricted	Unanimity
Organization of American States Permanent Council	Regionally restricted	Supermajority
Organization for Security and Cooperation in Europe	Regionally restricted	Varies
African Union	Regionally restricted	Supermajority
Arab League	Regionally restricted	Majority*
Association of Southeast Asian Nations	Regionally restricted	Consensus**

*Only consensus decisions are binding; majority required for passage
**Some exceptions

The end of World War II resulted in a new wave of liberal institution building.[15] Along with the Bretton Woods institutions and the General Agreement on Tariffs and Trade (GATT), the United Nations was created to provide a more robust collective security arrangement than the League. The architects of the UN sought to eliminate some of the indecisiveness of the League Council by requiring only a supermajority (instead of unanimity) for Security Council votes, although the major victors of World War II— Great Britain, the United States, France, the Soviet Union, and China—were given vetoes over Security Council decisions. The Charter of the United Nations also sought to make member state collective security obligations more explicit and legally binding.[16] The UN Security Council was very active in international disputes during the second half of the twentieth century, becoming involved in one-quarter to one-third of all international crises, although the number of formal resolutions produced by the Security Council increased dramatically after the end of the cold war.[17]

15. See Ikenberry 2001.
16. See Goodrich 1947.
17. See Malone 2004; Wallensteen and Johanssen 2004.

A related trend is the consultation of regional political organizations for external authorization.[18] Virtually every region of the world has witnessed the creation of multilateral economic and political organizations, although clearly the European Union is the broadest and deepest of such organizations. These organizations are consulted less frequently than the UN Security Council, but have nonetheless played central roles in prominent international disputes. For example, the OAS was highly critical of the U.S. invasion of Panama in 1989, and both the Arab League and the Organization for African Unity intervened diplomatically in a dispute between Morocco and Spain over Western Sahara in 1974. More recently, the African Union has played a direct role in political events surrounding the Darfur conflict. The Organization of Security and Cooperation in Europe has been active in discussing and addressing security issues in Asia and Europe, particularly in Eastern and southeastern Europe. Regional organizations have thus also been increasingly important in a number of events since the end of World War II.

As noted above, the fact that multilateral security organizations reflect the constellation of preferences among member states represents a fairly unique problem among international organizations, given that the types of issues considered by these organizations typically hold distributive consequences for member states. This problem is not present in many other types of international organizations, like trade dispute panels or international humanitarian tribunals, because the arbiters in these institutions are not usually state representatives. In multilateral security organizations, member states care about not simply whether an outcome or resolution to a crisis is normatively good, in the sense that peace prevails, but also are attentive to how outcomes directly affect their interests. The decisions to sanction a state for violation of an international agreement or to authorize regime change in a country carry costs and benefits that states feel in many ways. For instance, the regime change and political restructuring in Iraq following the 2003 war has far-reaching consequences for the distribution of oil wealth in the world, refugee flows in the region, and the distribution of power and overall stability of the Middle East. These consequences can fundamentally alter the balance of power in an entire region and contribute to reshaping international order.

The fact that voting members typically have strong personal stakes in the issues under consideration means that voting decisions reflect states' personal

---

18. Mansfield and Milner (1999) provide a summary of the economic trend. See also Lake and Morgan (1997) on regionalism in security affairs.

interests in how the international system should be ordered. At a practical level, this can make it quite difficult for an organization to deal with certain issues, such as the UN Security Council's limited ability to deal with superpower disputes during the cold war (cf. Goodrich 1965; Havilend 1965; Claude 1969). But for the purposes of this book, it points to the fact that organizational decisions will clearly reflect the "fingerprint" of member states' individual (and sometimes parochial) interests. In turn, a naive observer should be uncertain how much decisions are driven by members' self interest versus the merits of policies under consideration. From the point of view of the domestic or foreign observer, it is not clear what the decisions of an organization like the Security Council really means about the nature of a proposed policy intervention.

Decisions in multilateral security institutions are not simple products of preference aggregation. Rather, these decisions also involve deliberation, persuasion, and deal making (Voeten 2001). For instance, Security Council authorization for intervention in Haiti to reinstall ousted President Jean-Bertrand Aristide was likely made possible by U.S. concessions to China in economic matters (Malone 1998). Likewise, prior to the 2003 Iraq War, the Bush administration invested substantial resources attempting to persuade other Security Council members to explicitly authorize the use of force. In this sense organizational output often reflects considerable debate, negotiation, and perhaps side payments. Thus, in addition to reflecting states preferences, decisions may reflect material deal making rather than being altruistic responses to international security issues. This points toward a need for theoretical accounts of why multilateral security organizations matter to move beyond concepts such as neutrality, which in practice is not a characteristic of most multilateral security organizations, to a strategic theory of IO influence.

SCOPE OF THE BOOK

International political conflict and military events are central to the study of international relations. International conflict affects millions of people, directly and indirectly, through the loss of lives, the destruction of property and infrastructure, interruption of global economic patterns, and revision of the international distribution of power. Multilateral security organizations of the type addressed here are designed to deal with precisely these events. This book therefore focuses on international conflict.

As noted already, states commonly consult global and regional IOs during international crises or military disputes. Crises and military disputes are typified by one or more of the following events: an international conflict of interests, the perception of threat, diplomatic efforts to resolve the conflict, the threat or actual deployment of military forces, the use of military forces, reciprocation of threats or military actions. These events provide opportunities for states to craft foreign policy responses to particular threats or to build public support for foreign policy initiatives. This book argues that one way states do this is to consult multilateral organizations. This is not to say that crises and disputes are the only times governments interact with global and regional security forums. Governments certainly interact with IOs about issues of membership and procedures, development initiatives, and other foreign policy goals during less tense times, but times of crisis and imminent conflict represent the greatest threats to international peace and security.

Government behavior during crises may be coercive or defense. Coercive actions occur when the government of the state in question initiates a crisis or dispute with a demand of an adversary. Defensive responses occur when such demands are levied against the state in question. In both instances states have appealed to IOs for support and to approve their actions. For instance, the Clinton administration secured UN Security Council approval for its 1994 operation to reinstall the democratically elected president Jean-Bertrand Aristide to power. This crisis has elements of a coercive action, in that the United States demanded that the military junta of Raoul Cédras cede power.[19] In another example, Nicaragua requested a meeting of the UN Security Council in response to the United States taking a threatening posture in 1984 after reports indicated a cargo ship carrying Soviet MIG-21s was headed to Nicaragua. Nicaragua's appeal appeared to be a defensive move to justify its foreign policy position and condemn U.S. actions. In 1975 both Spain and Morocco issued appeals to the UN Security Council in order to stake out claims over the Spanish colonial territory of Western Sahara. In this case, the consultations had elements of coercion and defensiveness; Morocco's appeal was likely aimed at legitimizing its claims on the territory and forcing the Spanish to relinquish its rights. The Spanish appeal was a response to pressure mounting from the Moroccan claims amidst domestic political unrest at home (Hodges 1983; Zartman 1989). In each case, a sovereign country appealed to an international organization for a ruling on a conflict with another sovereign country—a behavior that begs analysis. This book argues that many of these consultations are driven by a common in-

---

19. That is, despite the crisis being triggered by the military junta, the United States sought support for demands it made of the junta.

centive to build domestic and international political support for state policy and that the degree to which this is accomplished depends on organizational structures and decisions.

OUTLINE OF THE BOOK

This book presents a rationalist, game theoretic explanation for why states often seek IO approval during international events. The book has two central goals—one theoretical and one empirical. The theoretical goal is to build on the limited research about the interplay between international organizations and domestic politics. Although much work has been conducted about the relationship between international economic agreements and organizations and domestic politics,[20] we know relatively little about the incentives leaders consider when seeking the approval of multilateral security organizations. Further research in this area is critical for several key reasons.

First, multilateral security organizations are, according to traditional perspectives on IOs, the least likely type of IO to broadly affect state behavior, because they deal in the "high politics" realm of security affairs. Moreover, security matters tend to have severe distributive consequences for member states, which means that political battles within IOs may have important consequences for the ultimate ordering of the international system.

Second, recent work has focused on identifying a number of indirect mechanisms through which IOs may influence behavior despite lacking robust enforcement power. Specifically, public opinion is one of these indirect channels, though there is still limited theoretical understanding of the operation of this channel. In light of anecdotal evidence that leaders are often attuned to how the rulings of multilateral security institutions affect domestic politics, it is important to conduct a more thorough investigation.

Third, there is very little dialogue between scholars that study political behavior and those that study international relations. Yet theories of domestic constraints on foreign policy decisions, which often rely on assumptions about the nature of citizens' knowledge, attention, and reaction, are quite common in international relations. This book self-consciously engages this link and, while not providing the ultimate statement about the complementarities of these approaches, will provide some theory and evidence as to the interplay between domestic opinion and foreign policy behavior.

---

20. For example, Putnam 1988; Milner 1997; Mansfield, Milner, and Rosendorff 2002; Vreeland 2003; Reinhardt 2003; and Dai 2005. See also Pevehouse 2005 on democratization and Carrubba 2009 on regulatory regimes. Drezner 2003 provides a good review.

The empirical goal is to provide several mutually reinforcing tests that can help discriminate between competing perspectives on why multilateral security IOs matter in world politics. This is critical because much of the evidence surrounding theories of why IOs matter is anecdotal or is consistent with multiple alternative explanations. For instance, the mere fact that states often ask for external approval is consistent with both a view that symbolic legitimacy is important and a view that IOs provide relevant information to domestic and foreign audiences. This book will develop a set of testable hypotheses and muster the proper data to discriminate between several alternative explanations that exist in the literature. I will show the strength of the informational approach by linking incentives to seek IO approval to the anticipation of the informational benefit it provides to domestic audiences.

To preview the rest of the book, chapter 1 examines existing perspectives on why states seek approval from multilateral security IOs. In particular, I argue that neither the so-called realist nor constructivist/legitimacy accounts adequately explain actual behavior and that an alternative should be developed. Prior to developing an alternative that views IO approval as a way to improve domestic support, it is useful to draw inspiration from work that investigates the various channels through which IOs influence domestic politics and the ways in which citizens learn from strategic sources of information. This discussion sets the stage for developing an alternative explanation for approval-seeking behavior that incorporates existing insights.

Chapter 2 presents a game theoretic account of information transmission from an IO to a domestic audience. In the model a government that cares about public support has the option of consulting a multilateral security organization for authorization for its foreign policies. This theory draws heavily on existing models of information transmission in political settings, but provides new claims that account for variation in observers' reactions across institutions, across time within the same institution, and across actors during the same event. The theoretical results generate predictions about public reaction to IO decisions, when and why governments consult multilateral security institutions, and how IO activity affects coalition building. Specifically, approval from an IO that is *ex ante* perceived as unlikely to offer approval is likely to be a boon for public support, while opposition from such an organization may often be discounted. The opposite is true for IOs that are perceived as *ex ante* predisposed to offer support. This creates incentives for governments to seek the approval of organizations that are seen as relatively "conservative" with their approval, as support from these organizations tends to improve public support for foreign policy, while opposition does not radically diminish public support. The degree to which organizations are more or less likely to grant approval likely stems from fixed features of the organization, such as membership and voting rules, and from member state statements and behavior proximate to a crisis. The former determine the degree to which the organizations' members are likely to have common interests and the difficulty of securing a supportive resolution or vote, while the latter can signal the foreign policy preferences of members and thus the likelihood that they will support a given initiative. The remaining chapters turn to empirical evidence of these mechanisms.

Chapter 3 analyzes the effect of organizational preferences on the decision of states in crises to consult international organizations. This chapter examines both the decision to consult the Security Council as well as the decision to consult relevant regional organizations. If external authorization is most likely to provide a boost to public support, in terms of signaling foreign policy appropriateness, when the organization is perceived as *ex ante* unlikely to support a policy, it follows that leaders have strong incentives to consult organizations that are considered "conservative" in their authorization. Moreover, the potential cost of opposition from such an organization is low, as it is a "noisy signal" of whether the policy is warranted. Using data on the relative preferences of states vis-à-vis multilateral security organizations, I examine whether states behave consistently with this logic. I also discuss qualitative evidence about the considerations of several U.S. presidents during consultations with multilateral security institutions.

Chapter 4 examines the effect of multilateral authorization on changes in U.S. public opinion during military events. Following the notion that the effect of organizational support depends on the constellation of preferences within an institution, the statistical tests in this chapter 4 account for the relative preference relationship between the United States and the UN Security Council as well as the United States and regional organizations. I also discuss more qualitative evidence, drawing on public opinion polling, supporting the idea that behavior consistent with what might be called organizational legitimacy is conditional on member state preferences within multilateral security organizations. I also present some descriptive evidence that the U.S. public does, in fact, have access to considerable information about the UN Security Council during times of foreign policy crisis, suggesting that while citizens may not, on average, know a great deal about foreign affairs, they are typically exposed to the type of information required for the decision making posited in the model presented in chapter 2.

Chapter 5 analyzes the notion that multilateral signals may provide information to foreign audiences and tests implications for the decisions of allies to join states in crisis. Namely, foreign audiences are more likely to treat organizational decisions as signaling low costs and appropriate foreign policy when the organization is not biased in favor of the proposing state and when the audience views its preferences as aligned with the organization. In these circumstances, foreign audiences are more likely to believe that proposed foreign policies conform to their preferences, which in turn frees up the domestic constraints of potential allies. Anecdotal evidence confirms this logic. For instance, President George H. W. Bush desired UN Security Council support to placate Arab public opinion prior to the first Gulf War, which would help garner the support of moderate Arab states (Bush and Scowcroft 1998). The United States similarly sought OAS support during its intervention in Haiti in order to avoid being perceived as meddling in Caribbean and Latin American affairs and thus win support from other Latin American states (Malone 1998).

The conclusion returns to the larger debate about the role of IOs in international security affairs. The evidence in this book suggests that governments tend to seek external approval to improve domestic and foreign support for foreign policy. This effect is more likely as an organization is perceived overall as more independent from the state seeking approval and less likely to automatically confer support. This dynamic has important implications for how IOs matter in international affairs. If leaders desire public support for policies, it follows that they will often avoid policies that will never garner external approval and may moderate policy proposals in order to win that approval. In this way, IOs have an indirect influence on foreign policy behavior through the channel of public opinion. At the same time, this highlights the dual nature of IO authorization. On one hand, the threat of IO opposition may deter overly aggressive policies. But at the same time, once IO authorization is granted, it may facilitate coercion[21] or embolden leaders to pursue more aggressive strategies than the otherwise might.

Finally, the theory and evidence presented in this book bear directly on debates about the reform of IOs like the UN Security Council. The theory suggests that the value of these organizations lies not in their willingness to approve every action, but in their reputation as organizations whose approval is difficult to acquire but sometimes forthcoming for low cost and meritorious policies. I make a case for design proposals that maintain this reputation rather than those that make action easier, for the United States in particular.

---

21. Thompson 2006; Chapman and Wolford 2010.

1

THE VALUE OF MULTILATERAL
AUTHORIZATION

As noted in the introduction, history shows that governments have often sought the approval of international organizations when conducting foreign policy, at least since 1945 and the creation of the United Nations. This pattern of consultation is understudied, particularly given that the dominant paradigmatic approaches to international relations theory, especially the realist tradition, take sovereign authority and the quest for power and security as a predominant feature driving international behavior. Although states have not forfeited their right to make the final decisions regarding their own security, they have increasingly consulted multilateral, supranational institutions for authoritative statements regarding international conflict, which potentially opens the door for increased scrutiny, criticism, and opposition to their foreign policies. Existing paradigmatic views of international relations theory do not provide clear answers to why states would subject themselves to this scrutiny.

The UN Security Council is the largest and most prominent of multilateral, consultative security organizations, but regional organizations have fulfilled this role in a number of ways. At least since the writing of Immanuel Kant, philosophers, scholars, and policymakers have argued that international organizations and international law can act as a force for peace. International organizations are thought to socialize members to norms of "good behavior" and facilitate mediation and conflict resolution between states, all reasons for states to involve them in their disputes. But there are several reasons why approval seeking behavior is puzzling. First, despite arguments from advocates of strong international law, there is no clear legal obligation for states to "get a second opinion" or subject their foreign policies to scrutiny prior to action. Second, the organizations in question are frequently derided for lacking direct and robust enforcement power. States routinely act without the formal approval of an international organization but are rarely if ever punished, and compliance with multilateral security organization dictates and rules is very imperfect. Yet governments continue to behave *as if* getting approval is important and invest considerable effort to garner it.

Two recent and prominent examples illustrate both the legal ambiguity of IO authorization as well as the lack of effective punishment mechanisms, especially for powerful states. In 1999, the United States initiated a bombing campaign against Serbian forces operating in Kosovo. The campaign took place with the cooperation and consent of NATO allies, but was criticized by many as illegal because it was prosecuted without a mandate from the UN Security Council (Roberts 1999). Likewise, the 1984 invasion of Grenada was roundly criticized by the Organization of American States and its member states, despite the fact that the United States was granted authorization from the Organization of Eastern Caribbean States (Beck 1993). In both cases, the United States and its allies argued that they had the requisite legal authority to carry out the respective actions. In neither case did the United States suffer serious sanctions in response to their actions, although in both cases it behaved as if garnering some sort of formal "stamp of approval" from an international organization was important, even if to provide some thin veneer of political cover. To some degree, the legality of many such actions appears to be in the proverbial "eye of the beholder," in the sense that strict proponents of international law argue against the legality of actions receiving multilateral opposition, while proponents of such policies often argue that overlapping and somewhat redundant institutional authorization provides the necessary legal authority.

There are, of course, a variety of views on the importance and effectiveness of international organizations within broader international relations theory. This chapter examines some of these and makes the case for a more strategic theory of states' interactions with multilateral security organizations. First, I address the implicit "null hypothesis" of work on international security organizations, namely, the realist claim that multilateral security IOs matter little for state behavior because they lack direct enforcement power. This claim simply does not match the evidence, in that states invest a considerable amount of effort to get the approval of these so-called "meaningless" organizations. Perhaps more importantly, this view neglects more indirect mechanisms of influence, such as the channel of public opinion. Because public support at home and abroad helps states accomplish their broad goals, compliance with institutional edicts may have more to do with the accompanying political benefits rather than with the strength of enforcement power.

Second, I assess the legal status of UN Security Council authorization as well as other international organizations. Scholars have noted a general trend toward increasing legalization in international affairs, pointing to developments in international dispute settlement and international human rights law (cf. Goldstein et al. 2000; Keohane, Moravscik, and Slaughter 2000; Abbott et al. 2000; Simmons 2000). As noted above, however, the legal status of authorization for the use of force is somewhat ambiguous, and although states frequently attempt to justify their behavior in legal language, the need for legal consistency is not a sufficient explanation for approval seeking (Voeten 2005). It is far from clear that increased legalization extends to the "high-politics" realm of security affairs, at least in so far as it applies to the need to acquire multilateral consent for foreign policies.

A third view, drawing inspiration from constructivism, is that IO approval matters because it provides symbolic legitimacy; indeed, even the act of consulting an IO may provide some legitimacy if it is seen as the procedurally appropriate thing to do (Hurd 2007).[1] This view also does not fully explain the evidence, in that governments seem to pick and choose when they consult international organizations, and the legitimacy perspective does not explain considerable variation in the effects of institutional activity. This view is also vulnerable to a theoretical critique: if we only are able to know IOs are legitimate when states act as if they are it may be difficult to disentangle the true causal mechanisms underlying a legitimacy effect. In other words, legitimacy is defined by the very acts we hold up as evidence of a legitimacy effect, establishing a definition that may be difficult to falsify.

A fourth view, which I build on in chapter 2, is that IO activity can provide information to audiences that are important to governments. That is, IO authorization can provide valuable political cover for governments considering controversial and possibly threatening foreign policies. Not all IOs are equipped to provide this cover, however. The usefulness of multilateral organizations for political cover depends on the informational content of their decisions. This perspective helps explain the selectivity with which

---

1. Franck (1990) develops a similar argument, and this line of reasoning bears some resemblance to Chayes and Chayes's work on compliance (1993, 1995).

21

governments appeal to IOs as well as the varying effects of IO decisions. This view adds to and extends recent work in a rationalist tradition that locates the importance of multilateral security organizations in their ability to alter the incentive structures of governments (e.g., Fang 2008; Thompson 2006, 2009; Voeten 2005). Because IOs may influence domestic and international politics in important ways, their decisions can have important ramifications for the strategic behavior of states.

After reviewing these alternative explanations, I discuss domestic constraints on foreign policy and the interaction of IOs and domestic politics, as covered in the recent literature. In particular, it is useful to consider the state of scholarship on public opinion and foreign policy in order to assess whether it is plausible that the public can draw inferences from IO decisions that in turn influence the degree to which citizens support their leaders. Although this book relies on a view of the public as generally uninformed, it assumes a base level of rationality that is plausible given existing studies of political behavior.

ENFORCEMENT AND INFLUENCE

Ever since E. H. Carr's critique of the League of Nations and interwar multilateralists (1939), scholars that identify themselves as realists have tended to dismiss international organizations as important actors in world affairs. Perhaps most famously, Kenneth Waltz labeled IOs "epiphenomenal," referring to the idea that they simply represent the power and interests of important states (Waltz 1979). In writing in the mid-1990s, John Mearsheimer (1995) alluded to the "false promise" of IOs, reflecting substantial skepticism about the pacific effects of institutions.[2] Notably, Mearsheimer pointed out that IOs should be least influential in the area of international security, since the primary goal of states is to preserve their own security. From this point of view, international organizations like the UN should have little effect on states' foreign policy behavior, serving rather as convenient window dressing for the enforcement capabilities of powerful states.

This view is certainly compelling, particularly given the history of global security institutions. The first truly large-scale attempt at collective security, the League of Nations, was formed in the aftermath of World War I with the

---

2. Mearsheimer's argument is compelling in many ways and is likely correct on many points. In particular, the conventional Kantian view of IOs as forces for peace neglects many strategic considerations of states (cf. Chapman and Wolford 2010). However, the theory in this manuscript points to one way organizations may influence state strategy without independent enforcement power.

goal of preventing future wars by mediating conflicts between states and facilitating collective responses to acts of aggression. The League was initially championed by President Woodrow Wilson, but the United States failed to join the League because of domestic isolationist sentiment manifested in Congress. Without the presence of the United States, who emerged after its late entrance in World War I as a rising superpower, the League Council was left with four permanent members: the United Kingdom, Italy, Japan, and France.[3] Notably, the League Council operated on a unanimous voting principle, which gave the four permanent members and others veto power over initiatives. As a result, it was powerless to intervene in response to the major aggressors of the interwar period—Italy, Germany, and Japan—and its legacy demonstrates a futility that many attribute to the lack of independent enforcement capability. The failure of this early attempt led to Carr's critique (1939) of advocates of international law and organization as "utopian" and helped refocus scholarship on the strategic and material interests of statecraft, rather than on normative concerns.

At first glance the UN seems to be very similar in design to the League. In its early years, optimism about the new postwar organization resulted in some involvement in the affairs of superpowers, such as Council discussions during the 1948 Berlin Blockade. The Security Council authorized military action in the Korean War, although notably in the absence of Soviet representation, as the Soviets boycotted the 1950 session. The cold war reduced the ability of the council to intervene in disputes involving the United States or USSR, but in the 1960s and 1970s the council played a part in disputes in the Middle East, Africa, and Southeast Asia. Indeed, the distribution of Security Council resolutions over its lifetime is heavily skewed away from the five permanent members' areas of direct interest (Wallensteen and Johanssen 2004), and the general perception of the organization during the cold war was that it was paralyzed by the opposing vetoes of the United States and USSR, supporting the view that IOs are impotent in cases in which they do not possess the capacity to enforce their mandates. When great powers are aggressors, enforcement is unlikely, although some have noted that formal multilateral opposition can limit cooperation and raise the costs of conducting foreign policy, even for powerful states (Voeten 2005; Hurd 2007).

The end of the cold war ushered in a new area of optimism regarding multilateral cooperation in general and the Security Council in particular. The council achieved remarkable consensus in 1990–1991, authorizing the

---

3. Germany later became the fifth permanent member, but withdrew in 1933 after Adolph Hitler was elected chancellor.

expulsion by force of Iraqi forces from Kuwait. The council also authorized a number of peacekeeping missions in the 1990s, as well as U.S. intervention in Haiti in 1994. However, mixed success in other cases throughout the 1990s weakened initial post–cold war enthusiasm. The 1999 circumvention of the Security Council by the United States in the Kosovo conflict, and the more unpopular decision in 2003 to conduct the Iraq War without explicit authorization, resulted in renewed charges of institutional impotence. Moreover, these events seemed to echo the claims of Carr and later scholars, who underscored the fundamental nature of state power and interests over institutions and international law.

The emphasis on enforcement that emerges from realist approaches to understanding international organizations has sound theoretical basis, even prompting scholars to assert the general principle that the "depth of cooperation" of any international agreement is proportional to the punishment required to maintain cooperation (Downes, Rocke, and Barsoom 1996, 385–87). In other words, the more an agreement or institution requires states to change their behavior, the stronger the agreement or institution's enforcement mechanism must be to ensure compliance. Combining this argument with Mearsheimer's insights, since no states are willing to forfeit their sovereignty over their security to multilateral institutions, and since those institutions lack enforcement power independent of the cooperation of states, most foreign policy behaviors in security affairs will go unpunished by multilateral institutions and, in turn, the presence of such institutions will do little to fundamentally alter state behavior.

The problem with this line of thinking is that there is an implicit assumption that incentives can only be altered by some hard punishment mechanism, but of course IOs like the UN rarely operate in this manner. The UN does establish some formal rules about appropriate uses of force and threats to international security, and the Security Council will routinely meet to discuss and debate alleged violations of these rules. However, the Security Council does not immediately dispatch a police force or fine the offending parties. Rather, it operates as a coordination mechanism for channeling state response (Voeten 2005) and it provides information to foreign (Thompson 2006) and domestic (Chapman 2007) publics. All of these mechanisms can, of course, alter incentives surrounding foreign policy, but are quite different than direct enforcement.

The realist focus on hard enforcement thus neglects some critical avenues of influence. As Voeten (2005) and others have pointed out, failure to obtain Security Council sanction can raise the costs of foreign policies by stimulating international opposition, and failure to obtain support from key domestic actors can make political life and the prosecution of successful foreign policy very difficult for leaders. Leaders consider these costs and craft their multilateral diplomatic strategies taking them into account. Assessing the magnitude of impact of these considerations on the aggressiveness or characteristics of foreign policy initiatives can be difficult, as it requires a counterfactual assessment of how policy might be aimed differently in a world without multilateral security organizations, but we can look for evidence of these mechanisms by examining domestic and international support for foreign policy initiatives under a range of circumstances.

LEGAL OBLIGATION

One alternative to the pessimistic realist view of IO influence in security affairs focuses on the increased legalization of the use of force in the twentieth century.[4] Although the international system has seen an increase in highly legalized international institutions, such as the World Trade Organization or European Union, there is still considerable disagreement over the legal ability of organizations like the UN Security Council to limit the use of force. Moreover, practical design matters have prevented the UN and like organizations to establish, in practice, the ability to become neutral legalistic arbiters over the appropriate use of force.

Each state that is a signatory to the UN charter ostensibly agrees to the various provisions of the charter, including the Chapter VII stipulations about the use of force. However, there is little about UN Security Council decisions that resembles those of a legal institution (Voeten 2005). They rarely, for instance, rule on the basis of existing precedent or on the letter of the law. In fact, the law regarding what constitutes a "threat to international peace and security," as represented by the language in Chapter VII of the charter, is too vague to make Security Council action "automatic" in the event of a particular international event. Instead, the decision to take action in response to a threat and the degree of response is determined by member states, which, in practice, can be read as the permanent five members (P-5), who each possess a veto over resolutions of the Security Council.[5] The fact that these five powerful states drive Security Council decisions means that

---

4. For discussions relating to the UN, see Wedgewood 2003; Roberts 1995, 2003; and Arend and Beck 1993. On legalization in international relations more generally, see Keohane, Moravscik, and Slaughter 2000; Abbott et al. 2000; Goldstein et al. (2000).
5. In fact, to my knowledge, no resolution has ever been blocked by a majority of the rotating members if the P-5 are in agreement.

Security Council behavior is inherently political. Unlike the highly legalized WTO dispute settlement mechanism, which is presided over by expert
judges in international trade law, or other international regulatory regimes
like the European Court of Justice, the Security Council is presided over by
member states, who themselves usually have a stake in the response to an
international event. Security Council decisions are not based on precedent
or legal principles, but rather on the political interests of the voting members and their expectations about how policy outcomes will affect international order.

The fundamentally political nature of the UN Security Council implies
that at a basic level its decisions cannot be decoupled from power politics.
However, proponents of international law point to the legitimacy afforded
by Security Council approval and to the regularized custom of states seeking
Security Council sanction.[6] Setting aside the arguments about the sources
of legitimacy for the moment, the customary nature of seeking Security
Council authorization is highly contested (Glennon 2001, 2003). States do
not always seek Security Council sanction and frequently conduct their foreign policies without it when it is clear that one or more of the P-5 intend
to veto a proposed policy. This was certainly the case during the cold war,
during which the United States and Soviet Union repeatedly vetoed policies
that the other supported.[7] It remains the case today, as the United States
has circumvented the Security Council in a number of prominent cases in
which a threatened veto was public knowledge, including the 1999 Kosovo
conflict (in which Russia threatened to veto Security Council authorization)
and the 2003 Iraq War (in which France, Russia, and China each threatened
vetoes). The customary status of approval seeking is therefore far from obvi-
ous and does not constitute solid footing for the broader legal status of the
institutions.

More generally, many scholars view international legal obligations as
very weak. For instance, comparing international and domestic legal systems, Goldsmith and Levinson write:

> Out of deference to state sovereignty, international law is a "voluntary" sys-
> tem that obligates only states that have been consented to be bound, and thus
> generally lacks the power to impose obligations on states against their inter-
> ests. As a result, the content of international law often reflects the interests of

6. See Tharoor 2003; Slaughter 2003.
7. Schacter 1989.

powerful states. And to the extent that international law diverges from those interests, powerful states often interpret away or ignore it. (2008, 1793)

These problems are perhaps more pronounced for regional organizations, which are less prominent than their global counterpart and are less able to influence states outside their regional boundaries. Regional organization decisions are also typically driven by member states with their own biases, their legitimacy is not universally accepted due to the exclusivity of their membership, and the legal status of their authorization is less certain than that of the Security Council. Given the often contested status of international law and its limited influence in security affairs, legal obligation fails to explain the importance afforded to diplomatic efforts to secure multilateral approval from international organizations.[8]

SYMBOLIC LEGITIMACY

A number of scholars have recently claimed that IO authorization is coveted because it affords legitimacy to foreign policy actions. According to this view, seeking IO authorization is seen as the procedurally correct course of action for responsible members of the international system. IO authorization itself has become more legitimate over time because states continually consult organizations and as certain organizations become imbued with symbolic importance (Hurd 2002).

Although definitions vary, legitimacy usually refers to a normatively held belief that a rule or decision ought to be obeyed because it is the right thing to do, not because obeying that rule will result in beneficial consequences (cf. Hurd 1999, 2007; Franck 1990). Legitimacy can be thought of as a psychological property or as a social construct (Tyler 2006). As a psychological property, it refers to an individual's belief that a rule or institution is valid

---

8. This is not to say that consistency with international law is not a common reason given publicly by political leaders for approval seeking. Indeed, the need to conform to international law is often precisely the reason given by Western leaders for consulting and adhering to multilateral mandates. However, I argue that this reason is chosen precisely for the effect it is expected to have on public opinion—that is, to characterize approval as conveying information about the merits of policies. When leaders circumvent multilateral institutions, they often give the reason that decisions of these bodies are driven by the parochial interests of member states, and therefore are not reflective of the underlying policy merits. For instance, in 2003, the Bush administration criticized French opposition to Security Council authorization for war, while in 1990 President George H. W. Bush lauded the new world order represented by the power of international community to uphold international law prohibiting the invasion of Kuwait by Iraqi forces.

or fair. As a sociological construct, it refers to a jointly held belief among a group or individuals that an institution or rule ought to be obeyed (Suchman 1995). Legitimacy is important because it allows authority to influence actors through means other than material inducements and deterrents (Tyler 2006). For instance, Ikenberry (2001) argues that in the aftermath of the Second World War, the United States sought to create a legitimate international order because relying on coercion to achieve its foreign policy goals would be prohibitively costly. By reassuring European allies and by actively incorporating their input, the United States was able to signal benign intent and imbue the postwar order with a sense of legitimacy.

Because legitimacy is a social construct, the constructivist tradition in international relations theory has explored this mechanism more than other research programs. Constructivism adds important insights to the study of international governance by highlighting ways in which institutions influence actors in other than in strictly cost-benefit terms.[9] Constructivist approaches, in contrast to the economics-oriented logic of rationalist approaches, focus on how international organizations can create meaning (Wendt 1992) and define norms of appropriate behavior (March and Olsen 1998). Institutions and transnational connections may have important influences that supersede material concerns, such as in the area of disarmament movements, which have influenced the international discourse on nuclear proliferation (Risse-Kappen 1994; Tannewald 1999). Importantly, the nature of organizational culture means that IOs can "take on a life of their own," operating with their own agendas independent from states (Barnett and Finnemore 1999).

A "softer" variety of this literature has noted that while an institutionalist or microeconomic perspective might identify a range of equilibria upon which states might coordinate, ideas or shared expectations affect which of these equilibria is actually chosen (Garrett and Weingast 1993). March and Olsen (1998), in particular, distinguished between a "logic of consequences," by which actors are rational and engage in negotiation reflecting preferences and interests, and a "logic of appropriateness," by which actions are based on rules and norms. A stronger version of the sociological approach rejects a rationalist view of state interaction almost entirely, asserting that states are primarily social actors and that their identities and world views are shaped by their environment and interaction with others.

---

9. For example, Haas 1990; Kratochwil and Ruggie 1986; Wendt 1994; Finnemore 1996; Johnston 2001, 2003.

This perspective implies that multilateral security institutions can be effective at constraining states by virtue of their symbolic legitimacy (Hurd 2002)—a socially constructed concept that defines which courses of action are subjectively "right" or "wrong." The logic that IOs can create meaning or even strategically manipulate meaning (Johnston 2001) provides one explanation for why IO approval is so coveted—namely, it confers a status on the behavior of country (or group of countries) that makes it much less likely that the country will encounter widespread opposition.

In the context of global governance, legitimacy is central to the effectiveness of international laws and institutions. International organizations that are seen as legitimate are imbued with more power and influence and are more likely to be complied with than those whose authority is weak or who are perceived as tools of powerful states (Barnett 1997; Barnett and Finnemore 1999; March and Olsen 1998; Grant and Keohane 2005). Legitimacy is, in essence, one way international institutions can circumvent the problem of weak enforcement capability. That is, although violations of international law are typically enforced only through the actions of other states, who themselves face difficult cost-benefit decisions as to whether to enforce laws, legitimacy may compel states to comply simply because they view a law as fair or normatively just. States clearly behave *as if* it were important to garner the imprimatur of the Security Council or other regional organizations when conducting foreign policies ranging from economic sanctions to humanitarian intervention to the enforcement of nonproliferation treaties. Put differently, states continue to act as if it the Security Council itself is legitimate (Hurd 2002) and capable of conferring legitimacy on their foreign policies through its authorization. But this begs a fundamental question: how does an institution come to be regarded as legitimate?

The literature provides several answers. First, consistent with psychological literature that finds that legitimacy derives from decision-making procedures that are regarded as "fair," UN Security Council legitimacy may owe to the fact that it represents the consensus of the international community. Since it is comprised of heterogeneous members with widely varying foreign policy preferences, its decisions take into account international public opinion and signal the consensus of a diverse set of the most important powers in the international system. A related idea is that the UNSC is regarded as relatively neutral because of its heterogeneous membership (Thompson 2006), which is one characteristic frequently associated with legitimacy (e.g., Grant and Keohane 2005; Barnett and Finnemore 1999).

A second view is that the UN Security Council is symbolically important because powerful states have sought out its sanction in the past. Overtime, the behavior of states in the international system has imbued the organization with legitimacy (Hurd 2002, 2007), which prompts states to continue to seek its sanction for political cover. At the end of the day, legitimacy stems from the fact that states treat the organization as if it is legitimate, as evidenced by their desire to participate in and work through it (Hurd 2002).

Both these views are unsatisfactory. First, it is unclear why the Security Council, or any other organization for that matter, would be regarded as neutral or its decision-making procedures as fair. The UNSC was specifically designed to give certain states a disproportionate influence in world affairs, in a direct response to the perceived failings of the League of Nations in the interwar period (Goodrich 1947). Voeten (2005) further points out that the Security Council is exclusive and anti-majoritarian by design. The organization's decisions rest on the preferences of five veto-wielding members, each of whom may have a stake in the issues under consideration. Furthermore, the ten rotating members are unable to exert much leverage in voting (Winter 1996; O'Neill 1996), and at no time has a decision been held up by a block of nonpermanent members when there was consensus among the P-5. Decisions inherently reflect the preferences of member states, so although consensus may be difficult to reach on a given issue, it is far from clear that the organization will be viewed as neutral or unbiased in all cases. Particularly in cases in which the UN rejects a proposed resolution or in which permanent members signal a veto threat and deter a resolution, the organization may appear very biased, as it only requires the disapproval of a preference outlier in order for a veto to occur.

The second explanation ignores the fact that state behavior is endogenous to the perception of organizational legitimacy. Procedural multilateralism is not a choice that great powers are constrained to pursue because of institutional rules, but a foreign policy strategy. It may be true that great powers, particularly the United States after World War II, aimed to build the Security Council's legitimacy by actively participating in it, but this begs the question of why this creates a perception of legitimacy. Moreover, decisions to circumvent the institution, and therefore decrease its legitimacy according to this explanation, are taken with full understanding that foreign policy strategies can affect how the organization is perceived. Additionally, the decision to veto resolutions, a strategy undertaken frequently by the United States, the USSR, and China during the cold war on issues ranging from condemnations of Israel to the Soviet invasion of Afghanistan, might also undermine the legitimacy of the organization. Yet at the same time, the legitimacy of the organization is beneficial to these states when conducting their foreign policies, so states face mixed motives when it comes to interacting with the institution. The legitimacy perspective does not disentangle the strategic interests of states, and hence can only partially explain the various effects of institutional decisions on perceptions of legitimacy and on state behavior.

INFORMATION PROVISION

An alternative explanation for behavior consistent with the legitimacy perspective is that IO authorization provides information to domestic and foreign audiences. This work has centered on the Security Council's ability to authorize the use of force. According to this perspective, there are at least two features of the Security Council that enable it to provide credible information, making its approval valuable.

First, because Security Council decisions tend to be driven by five of the most powerful states in the system, affirmative decisions are a strong signal that the international community will not impose excessive costs on a state for its foreign policy actions. The P-5 are the states that are most likely and most capable to sanction a state for rogue policies. These countries are most likely to do so because they have the largest vested interest in the international system. They are most capable because they are all nuclear powers with significant military capacity and at least some degree of global reach. These states also face little incentive to authorize policies that they may eventually oppose, since authorization makes policy implementation more likely and false authorization would jeopardize diplomatic credibility in the future. Taken together, these factors imply that Security Council authorization, which requires agreement of the P-5, can act as an "elite pact" signaling that the international community is broadly supportive of a proposed policy and will not attempt to obstruct or impose additional costs on the proposing state (Voeten 2005).

A related alternative points to the heterogeneity of preferences amongst Security Council members. The P-5, along with any given ten rotating members (selected according to regional representation), represent a diverse set of interests over foreign policy. Since the Security Council is global in representation, aside from its exclusivity, its median member is likely to be closer to the median member of the entire international community. This means, in turn, that the Security Council may be perceived as relatively neutral, and thus more capable to communicate policy relevant information to foreign audiences. Powerful states can sometimes capitalize on this feature of the Security Council and use the institution's authorization to signal benign intent to foreign audiences who might otherwise fear aggressive intent (Thompson 2006). This view is consistent with those that point to neutrality and inclusiveness as features of legitimate institutions in world affairs (Grant and Keohane 2005; Barnett and Finnemore 1999).

A third informational view is that international organizations tend be designed to promote "good policies," or policies that are appropriate responses to the state of the world. Citizens want to elect leaders who will implement "good policies," but tend to know little about international affairs and are therefore imperfect judges of their leaders' competency. However, because citizens see IOs as generally favoring good policies, they can infer information about their leaders' competency or ability to craft and implement good policies from their leaders' behavior vis-à-vis IOs. The member states of organizations like the Security Council have very little interest in supporting policies that will disrupt world order, but do have an interest in supporting policies that address threats to world order. Competent leaders will generally consult IOs in order to demonstrate their competency, while incompetent leaders will avoid IOs in order to avoid a public rebuke that reveals their nature to their citizens (Fang 2008).

These perspectives go further in developing a theory of the strategic political behavior of leaders and IOs, but each has shortcomings. The first two theories generally suggest that it is always optimal to seek Security Council authorization, but cannot explain why it is sometimes seen as more or less important. They are also silent about the effects of IO opposition, or failure to obtain authorization, on public opinion. Both of these phenomena—the variable importance of IO authorization and the effect of failures on public opinion—are important to explain because they occur frequently. This is evidenced simply by the fact that states have consulted the UN Security Council many more times than they have received a favorable resolution. The third perspective develops the relationship between leaders and citizens, but makes potentially unrealistic assumptions about the motivations of IOs. As noted above, the policies considered by security organizations often have distributive consequences for member states, meaning that states have a vested interest in certain outcomes. This would, in many cases, preclude pure policy altruism or neutrality, which, according to these theories would limit the ability of these organizations to provide useful information to citizens. As I show in chapter 2 the information provision function of IOs need not be restricted to altruistic or neutral organizations; citizens can learn from IO decisions that come even from biased institutions.

THE IO–DOMESTIC POLITICS LINKAGE

A basic part of the claim that leaders seek IO approval for domestic reasons rests on the idea that domestic politics can act as a constraint on leaders. This idea has a long tradition in international relations scholarship,[10] but in its contemporary form, scholars have frequently assumed that domestic audiences can impose costs on their leaders, particularly in countries where there exist institutional channels for sanction or removal.[11] This, in turn, means that leaders are attentive to how their actions will be received domestically. Leaders anticipate likely public reactions and try to avoid policies that will provoke a domestic backlash[12] while looking for ways to demonstrate their competency or boost domestic support for foreign policy.[13] Of course, leaders also take efforts to publicize and popularize their policies when they most anticipate potential opposition and most desire public support.[14]

The need to satisfy domestic constituencies, in turn, plays a large role in international negotiations and bargaining (Putnam 1988). Leaders are constrained by domestic politics in making deals and may take positions or sign agreements in order signal intent to various constituencies.[15] At the same time, domestic constraints can provide incentives for compliance with agreements, as powerful domestic constituencies may oppose deviation from international regimes.[16] Recent experimental evidence, for instance, demonstrates that citizens tend to prefer policies that conform to international law, supporting the idea that domestic politics can have constraining effects on leaders' behavior.[17]

The notion that domestic politics can constrain foreign policy has led to the discussion of a variety of mechanisms through which IOs, even those

---

10. Doyle (1986) traces the idea back to Kant; Maoz, and Russet (1993), who articulate the alternative logics of normative and institutional constraint explanations for the democratic peace. See Milner (1997) for a statement of the linkages between domestic and international politics.

11. For example, Fearon 1994; Smith 1998; Bueno de Mesquita et al. 1999, 2003.

12. Schultz (2001b) makes the point that so-called audience costs will be difficult to observe for precisely this reason.

13. The literature on how leaders use foreign policy to boost public support is vast, but see Tarar 2006; Smith 1996, 1998; Derouen 2000; Dassel and Reinhardt 1999; and Miller 1995. Levy (1988, 1989) provides good reviews.

14. On when leaders may "go private" instead of making public threats or comments, see Baum 2004. For distinguishing the patriotism and opinion leadership hypotheses, see Baker and Oneal 2001.

15. Mansfield, Milner, and Rosendorff 2002; Tarar 2001, 2005; Leventoglu and Tarar 2005.

16. Dai 2005.

17. Tomz 2007a.

with weak enforcement power, can indirectly influence leaders through domestic channels. For instance, human rights treaties, despite lacking enforcement power, may serve to shed light on and legitimate good human rights practices such that repeat offenders find it difficult to avoid opprobrium for their abuses (Hafner-Burton and Tsutsui 2005). International organizations may exert influence on domestic processes as well, by facilitating democratization (Pevehouse 2005) or by tying elites' hands to enact painful reforms (Vreeland 2003; Reinhardt 2003).

In short, the idea that IOs may influence state behavior in ways other than by exercising direct enforcement power has considerable theoretical and empirical backing at a macro level. The mechanism of influencing states through domestic constituencies appears to be a valid explanation of compliance with IOs in many areas, although with the exception of several experimental studies, we have little evidence that citizens are able to perform the tasks necessary to provide the threat of domestic sanction for either bad foreign policy or for failing to behave consistently with IO rulings.[18]

The lack of consistent findings about the micro-level foundations of domestic accountability and constraints is striking, as studies linking foreign policy behavior to domestic politics presuppose varying degrees of citizen knowledge and sophistication. How much do citizens actually know about foreign events and how much does it matter for their ability to sanction their leaders for implementing disagreeable policies? The literature offers both optimistic and pessimistic answers. The pessimists, especially early writers like Walter Lippman and Gabriel Almond, viewed the public as ill-informed about foreign affairs and as a potentially damaging force to the conduct of good foreign policy.[19] This perspective is based on poll findings, dating at least back to seminal study of Campbell et al. (1964), which showed little stability in attitudes about foreign affairs and little practical knowledge about international events. From the pessimist's point of view, the public *writ large* is simply not capable of making sophisticated political judgments about foreign affairs, and thus is largely incapable of playing a rational constraint role upon its leaders.

Later writers reached more optimistic conclusions about the public. In particular, Page and Shapiro made several contributions to the literature

---

18. As noted above, Tomz (2007a, 2007b) provides experimental confirmation that U.S. citizens prefer behavior consistent with international law and of the audience costs mechanism.

19.See Lippman 1925 and Almond 1950. Holsti 1996; Aldrich et al. 2006; and Baum and Potter 2008 provide good reviews. See also Page and Bouton 2006.

drawing on large amounts of survey data showing that, in the aggregate, public attitudes regarding foreign policy are both stable, in the sense they are not prone to wild variation, and rational, in that they appear to respond in predictable directions to foreign policy events.[20] More recent studies have found that public opinion responds in expected ways to policy success (Gelpi, Feaver, and Reifler 2005–2006) and to the rate of casualties during military conflicts (Gartner and Segura 1998), further examples that public sentiment is often driven by international affairs.

Of course, the debate about whether ordinary citizens should be and are capable of playing a role in the formation of foreign policy has much older roots. Scholars such as Rousseau and Kant talked of the virtues of public influence on foreign policy and seemed to believe in the ability of citizens to influence their leaders in reasonable directions. Others, including many of the founding fathers of the United States, saw public opinion as highly variable and susceptible to fads, opting to place more influence over foreign affairs in the U.S. Senate than in the House, with more frequent elections and narrower constituencies. Even Alexis de Tocqueville, who is perhaps best known for praising the civic virtues of American democracy, suggested that democratic diplomacy may be guided by "impulse rather than prudence" (Tocqueville 1958, 243–45, quoted in Holsti 1996).

In making the link from public opinion to its effect on actual political outcomes, Aldrich, Sullivan, and Borgida (1989) suggest that three criteria are necessary for public opinion to effect electoral outcomes and foreign policy. First, public opinion must be coherent. Second, citizens must access these coherent attitudes when deciding vote choice. Third, political parties (and the candidates they put forth) must have distinct foreign policy platforms that allow citizens to distinguish between choices. Aldrich and colleagues, in a more recent review of the evidence ranging from Almond's and Lippman's writings to 2006, conclude both that "these three criteria have often—though not always—been met since the collapse of the bipartisan foreign policy consensus during the Vietnam War" and that "a mounting body of evidence suggests that the foreign policies of American presidents—and democratic leaders more generally—have been influenced by their understanding of the public's foreign policy views" (2006, 33). In other words, studies of American public opinion, and findings about the behavior of democracies more generally, support the notion that the public can play a constraining role on government behavior.

20. See Page and Shapiro 1982, 1992; Page, Shapiro, and Dempsey 1987.

The role of domestic politics in foreign policymaking obviously varies across countries with different institutional channels for translating preferences into policy. Democracies have the most open channels through which public attitudes affect policy, through regular elections, referendums, plebiscites, and other less formal means of influencing elected officials. The same channels are absent to a greater or lesser degree in nondemocratic countries depending on their internal makeup. For this reason, the domestic benefits of external approval are most likely to pertain to democracies.

TOWARD A STRATEGIC THEORY OF APPROVAL SEEKING

Ultimately, data analysis can help determine whether leaders seek approval for domestic reasons. However, we must first develop a theory of the patterns we should expect to find in order to construct appropriate tests. Politicians are no doubt strategic in their conduct of foreign policy, and politicians across countries and across time frequently find themselves in the position of desiring strong public support for their foreign policies. Citizens, for their part, face strong incentives to look for information that can help them judge whether they should support their leaders' policies. Yet we know from extant studies that the degree to which citizens can learn from external sources depends on the strategic incentives of those sources. This all implies that approval-seeking behavior involves a complex dynamic between citizens' beliefs and strategies, politicians' strategies, and the behavior and activity that takes place in international organizations. Chapter 2 turns to a theory that analyzes these dynamics.

2

INSTITUTIONS, MEMBER STATE BIAS, AND INFORMATION TRANSMISSION

Given that IOs can sometimes provide important information to domestic audiences that can sometimes boost support for foreign policies, when are leaders most likely to seek IO approval? What explains why institutional decisions are sometimes treated as important by domestic audiences and how does this influence foreign policy? In the previous chapter I made the case that existing theories that point to the membership or decision-making rules of multilateral security organizations cannot adequately explain the conditions under which organizational decisions will be regarded as important, since these decisions inherently reflect the biases of member states. Legitimacy-based explanations, on the other hand, fail to take into account the variable nature of legitimacy owing to the strategic behavior of states. This chapter develops an alternative explanation rooted in rationalist explanations of information transmission.

To preview the argument, citizens, both domestic and those in foreign countries, face a classic asymmetric information problem, in that they know little about outcomes of foreign policies proposed by their leaders or other states. However, citizens can look to a variety of sources to help them decide whether or not to support these policies. These sources include the media, opposition parties, and the leader proposing the policy. International organizations are another source of information citizens can look to when making decisions about foreign policy.

However, given that the states that make up international organizations often have a distributive stake in policy outcomes, and that organizational decisions reflect member state preferences, citizens will not always take institutional decisions at face value. Instead, citizens weigh their perceptions of organizations' preferences against the content of the decision or message when forming their opinion. This assumes only that citizens are uncertain about foreign policy outcomes and that citizens have some perception of organizational neutrality or bias. For the time being we do not have to assume that citizens' perceptions are correct, although if these perceptions are to influence policymakers they must be more or less consistent across a population. In later chapters I discuss the plausibility of this assumption, as well as whether we can derive an adequate proxy measure of how citizens regard international organizations.

In chapter 1 I laid out a general critique of the literature investigating how institutions affect states' foreign policy behaviors. In particular, much of the literature sets aside the preference-driven behavior of institutional members and instead assumes a more or less static set of preferences within given institutions. This chapter relaxes this assumption to examine how preference-driven behavior affects information provision from institutions and, in turn, how this might affect foreign policymaking.

The following pages discuss a game-theoretic model that investigates the conditions under which an audience will regard the decision of a multilateral organization as conveying *policy-relevant* information, or information about the likely costs and merits of foreign policy actions. In doing so, the model also addresses the conditions under which leaders have incentives to consult multilateral institutions. In the model, a domestic audience is uncertain about likely foreign policy outcomes and learns from the behavior of its leader and from the decision of an international institution. The institution serves as a device for a "rationally ignorant" domestic audience to learn about the consequences of their leader's actions. However, the degree to which institutional decisions affect the behavior of the public varies with the *preferences* of member states and the *content* of signals sent by the institution. In general, institutional decisions will be treated as more legitimate, from the point of view of the domestic audience, when those decisions go against the known biases of member states.

While this result is common in game-theoretic models of information transmission,[1] it has been largely neglected in applications to international

1. On the value of biased information, see Kydd 2003; Calvert 1985; and Lupia and McCubbins 1998.

organizations. This logic suggests that the perception of institutional legitimacy is *conditional* on member and observer preferences and strategic behavior. The ability of institutions to affect foreign policy decisions through providing legitimacy is thus conditional on these preferences and behavior.[2]

Another way of stating this conclusion is that citizens' attitudes will be moved by institutional decisions when they believe that those decisions communicate *policy-relevant* information. Decisions that conform to the perceived biases of member states may or may not convey information about the merits of a policy, from the point of view of citizens. However, under certain conditions IO decisions allow citizens to learn about whether proposed foreign policies will yield preferable outcomes. In these cases, we will see citizens behaving as if institutions are authoritative or legitimate because their decisions inform citizens about the merits of proposed policies.

As an illustration, consider the following stylized example. Suppose that when evaluating foreign policy, citizens have an *ex ante* prior belief of α that the probability that any given policy is good, and a prior belief of $1-\alpha$ that a policy is bad. Suppose also that citizens have some perception about the predisposition of the UN Security Council and its attitudes toward supporting the use of force. Let the probability that the UNSC, or its most distant vetoing member, is generally biased against supporting the use of force be β and the prior probability that the UNSC is biased in favor of the use of force be $1-\beta$. Finally, assume that citizens have some conditional expectation about whether the UNSC will support "good" and "bad" initiatives, given this bias. Let p(support good policy | anti-force) $= q$ and p(support good policy | pro-force) $= r$, where $r > q$. Also, let p(support bad policy | anti-force) $= p$ and p(support bad policy | pro-force) $= s$, where $s > p$. Finally, let p(oppose good policy | anti-force) $= w$ and p(oppose good policy | pro-force) $= z$.

If recent activity has primed citizens to believe that $\beta = 1$ and $p = 0$, or that the UNSC is generally against the use of force *and* that the probability of *supporting* a bad proposal involving the use of force given that it generally against the use of force is nil (and, by extension, the probability of opposing a bad policy is 1), then by Bayes's rule rational citizens should be able to make the following assessments:

---

2. In this sense, the model is consistent with Voeten's realist view of institutions as forums for bargaining (2001). Although this model focuses on the informational role of institutions, the issue of power is especially relevant to the credibility of signals of opposition (more below). The effect of member state preferences on policy effectiveness has received considerable attention in the IMF and IFI literature (Stone 2004; Thacker 1999; Dreher, Sturm, and Vreeland 2009).

$p(\text{policy is good} \mid \text{UNSC supports}) = (\alpha q)/(\alpha q + (0)(1-\alpha)) = 1$
and
$p(\text{policy is good} \mid \text{UNSC opposes}) = (\alpha w)/(\alpha w + z - z\alpha) > 0$

In other words, support under such a set of circumstances should give citizens a posterior belief that a policy is good with certainty, while opposition does not eliminate the possibility that a policy is good. In fact, opposition under these circumstances could result in a very high posterior probability that a policy is good—that is, not discourage citizens' enthusiasm for a given policy—depending on the value of citizens' prior beliefs about the policy and their perception of the likelihood of opposition from a biased UNSC.

Note also that the starting values for the perception of the UNSC and its likelihood of supporting and opposing bad policies are entirely plausible. That is, if the UNSC is generally perceived to be against authorizing the use of force, we would intuitively expect it to oppose most bad policies and oppose some policies that are "good" from the point of view of the average observer. The *ex ante* perception of the institution's bias may come from media accounts, revealed statements made my permanent members, or past behavior. The key point is that these perceptions shape what citizens should think about policy, if they have some prior perception of the institution's predisposition.

This general idea has implications for several areas of interest to international relations scholars. First, the model developed in this chapter predicts that public opinion–conscious leaders face strong incentives to consult and gain the support of institutions whose members tend to disagree with them in order to bolster domestic support for policies.[3] Leaders also face incentives to avoid the disapproval of overly revisionist institutions, which will tend to reduce public support for policies. This provides a domestically oriented informational rationale for why leaders approach international institutions for authorization when conducting foreign policy.[4]

Second, the model provides an informational logic for previously unexplained variance in perceptions of legitimacy. Institutional legitimacy is not constant; it varies as a function of durable features of institutions, such as membership and decision-making rules, across context, as foreign policy preferences will vary with the type of issue under consideration, and across observers, who may hold very different preferences about foreign policy. It

---

3. See Dai 2005 for a theory of domestic incentives for compliance. For examples of other work linking domestic politics and IOs, see Drezner 2003; Pevehouse 2005; and Vreeland 2003.
4. Thompson (2006) suggests alternatively that working multilaterally primarily serves to signal benign intent to foreign audiences.

is very possible to have different observers appear to view the same institution or decision with different degrees of legitimacy, just as it is possible for the same observer to view the same institution with varying degrees of legitimacy over time. This is possible because perceptions of institutional biases partially determine how observers react to institutional decisions.

Third, the following theoretical model sheds light on interesting issues in institutional design. The model demonstrates that institutions that are seen as overly revisionist tend to be effective at constraining expansive foreign policies, while institutions that seen as more conservative may often have their opposition discounted as "cheap talk." However, the latter institutions are well equipped to convince audiences to support policies by granting their authorization. While institutions may vary in their "conservativism" across issue contexts, fixed membership and voting rules can make some institutions more or less conservative, suggesting an important link between institutional rules and effectiveness. Under many conditions international institutions can constrain foreign policymakers through the indirect channel of public opinion. Leaders often face incentives to choose policies that can garner the support of international institutions, which limits available policy options.

In the following section I discuss information transmission theories more generally. Next I discuss the core assumptions of the theory and its key conclusions. In the interest of accessibility, the discussion of the model is completely nonformal and I refer technically interested readers to the appendix at the end of this chapter. After the theoretical discussion I discuss the implications of the model for three areas of scholarly interest: the determinants of procedural multilateralism, public opinion and multilateralism, and the design of international institutions.

SIGNALING AND CHEAP TALK IN INFORMATION TRANSMISSION

In order to explore the informational dynamics underlying a body like the UNSC, it is useful to consider the findings of general information transmission models. Although such models come in a variety of forms, they generally start from the assumption of asymmetric information—that is, a situation in which at least one actor knows more information than other actors in a strategic setting. The less informed actors hold prior beliefs about the state of the world at the beginning of the game and then receive a signal from the more informed actor that may or may not allow her to update her prior beliefs about the state of the world.

There are two broad types of signals in games of strategic information transmission. The first is a costly signal, which occurs when the actor with private information incurs a cost for sending a signal (or takes an action which may commit it to incurring a cost). For example, this signaling device is commonly used in models in which armed belligerents have private information about their resolve to understand how conflict can be avoided or how coercion occurs. An example of a costly signal would be burning bridges, as it commits the adversary to continuing on a forward trajectory and eliminates the possibility of backing down.[5]

The second type of signal is known as a cheap talk signal. A cheap talk signal is a verbal statement that doesn't necessarily commit the actor issuing it toward a particular course of action or invoke a cost. An example would be issuing diplomatic statements that are not necessarily costly to break. To be sure, there may be negative consequences for frequently acting against one's prior statements, such as the loss of diplomatic credibility (Sartori 2005), but this is a negative consequence that is incurred in the future when the state needs to invoke its reputation in order to get what it wants.

The following model incorporates elements of both costly signals and cheap talk, but for most of the discussion I focus on the cheap talk signals that are issued by the member states of IOs. This establishes a "difficult case" for IO influence, because realist scholars often dismiss these institutions as simply forums for debate, with no real teeth and therefore little influence on state behavior. Statements or resolutions issued by international institutions can be considered "cheap" if there is not a strong incentive binding states to act subsequently in accordance with their decisions. For instance, a threatened veto by France in the Security Council does not automatically compel it to take military action against states that proceed with their policies outside of a Security Council framework. It may compel France to avoid cooperation with such states for a period of time out of fear of alienating domestic audiences. But in general, statements of opposition or support do not immediately incur costs for member states, but rather serve to make their preferences known.

BIAS AND NEUTRALITY IN INFORMATION TRANSMISSION

There are two broad, and at first glance contradictory, lessons provided by cheap talk models: neutral sources of information are useful and biased sources of information are useful. Studies of the informational role of committees, for instance, conclude that policy *neutrality* results in "informa-

---

5. Within costly signals there is a distinction between sunk costs and tying hands (Fearon 1997).

tional efficiency" (e.g., Gilligan and Krehbiel 1988, 1990). These models are concerned with how a principal (a legislature) can learn from the decision of an agent (a committee) with private information. The principal has incentives to select an agent whose preferences align to the principal's or does not *ex ante* prefer a certain type of policy, as the agent will send signals that are either in the principal's interest or that advocate the policy that is best suited for the issue at hand (e.g., Bawn 1995; Gilligan and Krehbiel 1990). Applied to international institutions, this logic suggests that a neutral institution is best equipped at providing information to uninformed observers.

A second finding is that biased sources of information are useful (cf. Kydd 2003; Calvert 1985). Bias allows the agent to send credible signals, in the sense that the agent has incentives to send signals that accord with its own bias. When the agent acts against those incentives, the principal is able to update its beliefs about the agent's private information. In both cases, the ability to influence a principal's beliefs about the agent's private information depends not only the preferences of the agent but also on the preference relationship between the principal and agent and the incentives of the agent to reveal private information (e.g., Lupia and McCubbins 1998; Farrell and Gibbons 1989). Of course, an agent whose preferences are perfectly aligned with the principal is optimal when the principal is making decisions under uncertainty. However, this is often not possible in a wide range of political situations. When it is not possible to choose a dutiful agent with one's own preferences, the degree of bias in the agent's preferences may provide useful information.

One way to think of the role of IOs is as agents that can provide information about foreign policy. In many cases, these agents may appear very credible because they are largely autonomous and develop organizational preferences formed by policy-minded technocrats who care only about policy success (Abbott and Snidal 1998; Barnett and Finnemore 1999).[6] In other cases, institutions operate more as voting bodies, meaning that the policy preferences of members are likely to figure prominently into the institution's signals. Formal decisions ultimately hinge on the preferences of a pivotal member. This member is the vetoing member least likely to support the policy in a veto (or consensus) context, or the median voter in a majoritarian context.[7] Again, consider the French position regarding a second resolution authorizing the 2003 Iraq War. France's position was pivotal because it

---

6. But see Barnett and Finnemore 1999 on the pathologies of autonomous IOs.

7. The literature on IMF lending clearly makes this point. The United States, as the largest contributor, enjoys de facto veto power over IMF decisions. This affects lending credibility, as the United States is less likely to enforce conditionalities on allies or strategically important states (Stone 2004).

seemed the least likely to announce support for a resolution authorizing war.[8] By implication, if war was acceptable to France, it should also be acceptable to countries with less extreme preferences. This suggests that the perception of failure to obtain UNSC authorization is contingent on observers' beliefs about determinants of France's position, which could be policy merits or other features of French politics unrelated to the policy merits of war.

CITIZEN PERCEPTIONS AND INFORMATION TRANSMISSION

So while it may be optimal to rely on a purely neutral or altruistic source of policy information, it is often not viable in practice. However, there is a further requirement in order for the degree of neutrality or bias of member states to play any role in the legitimization process. Namely, citizens or observers must have at least some perception about the degree of neutrality or bias among key members of the institution. In the Security Council context, the key member is the member that is most distant from the state requesting authorization, as that is the member that must favor a policy in order for it to pass. If the most distant member favors the policy, then the remaining members, with preferences even closer to the proposer, should favor it as well. It follows then that if external authorization is to provide policy-relevant information, it must also be true that citizens hold some beliefs about the general foreign policy preferences of the member state driving a particular decision.

This is potentially a strong requirement for citizens. As noted in chapter 1, public opinion research in the United States generally finds that citizens are not very knowledgeable about international events, although public opinion in the aggregate appears to respond in predictable ways to a number of different events (Page and Shapiro 1992). However, as the following theory demonstrates, citizens may not need to know very much about foreign affairs in order to have an incentive to pay attention to and learn from IO signals.

One reason citizens may care about IO signals is that, generally speaking, domestic audiences prefer low-cost to high-cost foreign policies. This assumption underlies much of the democratic peace literature and dates back at least to Kant's writing in *Perpetual Peace*, in which he argued that since citizens pay the costs for foreign policy, they will generally be reluctant to

8. France was the first country to announce its intent to veto such a resolution, followed shortly by Russia and China.

support aggressive or costly uses of force.[9] Of course, in order for the public to exercise any constraint on its government it must be able to make judgment about the costs of foreign policy. For instance, domestic audiences must link rising casualties, mounting taxation, and economic consequences to the foreign and military policies of their leaders. The mechanism of how the public imposes costs may be direct, through elections, or indirect, through dampening support for a democratic leader's general agenda.[10] The amount of costs the public imposes may vary across leaders and situations as well. The key point is that public concerns over the costs of foreign policies point toward a natural incentive to develop mechanisms to constrain leaders.

If the public is able to make reasonable *ex ante* inferences about proposed foreign policies it must be able to make some assessment of the various types of information it is exposed to. As I note above, an important component of this process is the formation of perceptions about the biases of different sources.[11] The public may develop perceptions of the relative bias of the media, opposition parties, and international organizations in order to interpret whether these sources should be trusted. This perception may not necessarily be correct and, in all likelihood, contains some considerable error, which I account for in the following theoretical model.

How plausible is it that citizens have access to information about the Security Council when forming opinions about foreign policy events? As an initial answer, consider the following evidence on the frequency of media reporting on the Security Council during the first Gulf War, the 1994 Haiti operation, the 1999 Kosovo campaign, and the 2003 Iraq War. These four events vary in terms of whether the United States consulted the UN Security Council, NATO, both the Security Council and NATO, or simply operated under a coalition of the willing. These events also vary in terms of whether a

9. See Doyle 1986 and Russett and Oneal 2001. Evidence in the United States shows that the public prefers defensive action over intervention (Jentleson 1992; Lian and Oneal 1996; Jentleson and Britton 1998) and has an aversion to casualties (Gartner and Segura 1998). Also see Eichenberg 2005 for a more recent review of this scholarship. Scholars of the constraining effects of democratic institutions build on this logic (e.g., Reiter and Stam 2002).
10. Compare with Brody 1991.
11. Lupia and McCubbins (1998) develop a detailed theory of how democratic institutions influence incentives for truth telling behavior and for the ability of citizens to draw proper inferences from the strategic behavior of a variety of political actors. In the context of multilateral security institutions, there are a variety of opportunities for actors to reveal their preferences through voting behavior or other foreign policy behavior, particularly because votes are difficult to enforce. While horse trading and strategic voting likely affect many votes in an institution like the UN Security Council, it unlikely citizens would know about these backdoor deals and therefore unlikely that this behavior would affect citizens' inferences about votes.

TABLE 2.1   Selected media coverage of the UN Security Council

EVENT COVERAGE, BY NEWSPAPER	NUMBER OF STORIES
Haiti (July–October 1994)	
NYT	39
USA Today	20
AJC	14
Total	73
Persian Gulf War (March 1990–January 1991)	
NYT	519
USA Today	128
AJC	35
Total	682
Kosovo (April–November 1999)	
NYT	68
USA Today	13
AJC	18
Total	99
2003 Iraq War (January 2002–April 2003)	
NYT	916
USA Today	245
AJC	207
Total	1,368

Note: AJC, Atlanta Journal-Constitution; NYT, New York Times.

security IO authorized military action and in severity. Table 2.1 displays the frequency of reporting across three major U.S. newspapers: the *New York Times*, the *USA Today*, and the *Atlanta Journal-Constitution*. The first two represent national newspapers of varying sophistication, while the last represents a major regional newspaper. The table provides only a rough snapshot of the nature of media coverage surrounding these events. One cannot directly compare the number of news stories across events because they cover different time periods, but it is clear that even for lower scale events, like the Haiti invasion, or for events that the Security Council does not authorize, like Kosovo, there is considerable media coverage across different types of print news outlets. Of course, large events, like the two Persian Gulf wars, are afforded an incredible amount of coverage. But the central point is that readers of these news sources, which probably represent samples of the public with varying degrees of interest and sophistication, have considerable exposure to information about the activity of international organizations during major foreign policy events. Citizens have the incentive, based on their preference for low-cost foreign policies, and opportunity, based on media coverage, to pay attention to IO decisions.

In later chapters I approach the problem of whether citizens can make reasonable inferences from the cues of IOs through empirical cross-validation. For example, in chapter 3 I look at whether citizens' assessments of presidential approval conform to what we would expect if they believe policies authorized by more conservative institutions are more legitimate. In chapter 4 I look at how we would expect governments to behave if they anticipate institutional decisions to have variable effects on public support, and in chapter 5 I look at how potential coalition partners should behave if this were true. These tests support one another and thus provide evidence for the informational explanation proposed here.

A MODEL INSTITUTIONAL INFORMATION TRANSMISSION

The following model is designed to investigate whether a potentially biased institution can influence state behavior by informing public attitudes. It also shows that the influence of multilateral security organizations need not be restricted to domestic audience, as others have pointed to the role of the UNSC in communicating legitimacy to the international community (Thompson 2006; Voeten 2005). In the interest of accessibility I present the model informally and relegate a more technical discussion to the appendix of this chapter.

Actors

The game has three actors: a leader (L), a public (P), and the pivotal member of a multilateral security organization (M). Rather than include multiple voting members, the preferences of the organization can be represented by a pivotal member whose vote is required in order for a resolution to pass.[12]

Sequence

The leader has the option of accepting the status quo policy, located at 0 on a unidimensional policy space,[13] proposing a policy unilaterally, or proposing a policy through the institution. If the leader proposes the policy multilaterally, the pivotal member signals "support" or "oppose." The public then

---

12. In a veto context this is the member who is least likely to vote yes, or the member with the most distant preferences. In a majoritarian context it is the median voter.

13. The key conclusions about preference distances driving outcomes apply if one were to allow the status quo to vary.

decides whether to support or oppose their leader. In the initial version, the public votes sincerely, in that they simply signal whether they prefer the policy to the status quo. If the leader proposes the policy unilaterally, the public decides whether to support or oppose their leader without observing any signal from the multilateral organization.

Utilities

Actors have an ideal policy along a dimension that represents deviations from the status quo. One interpretation of this setup is that policies that fall further to the right represent more extreme deviations from the status quo, or, more aggressive attempts to order the existing international order. One can interpret preferences as ranging from more "dovish" to more "hawkish" along this line. Actors prefer policies that fall closer to their ideal points than policies that fall further from their ideal points.[14]

All else equal, leaders prefer policies that have public support rather than those that do not. Leaders therefore pay a cost for domestic opposition, which can range from extremely small to extremely large. The costs of domestic opposition vary across types of countries according to domestic institutions. Leaders in democracies are likely to feel the largest costs for enacting policies that are publicly opposed, while leaders in regimes without institutional channels feel fewer costs. Of course, all leaders face the need to maintain popularity at home, and this may vary with other circumstances, such as the state of the economy.

Information

For simplicity, assume that the public is uncertain about the ultimate outcome of the policy proposed, although the leader and the pivotal member can anticipate this with certainty. Suppose the leader proposes some policy,

---

14. The assumption of unidimensionality effectively collapses the various preference dimensions that foreign policy might affect (e.g., economic relations, security) into one dimension that describes the distance between a policy and the status quo. This is a common simplification in ideal point settings. Studies of the dimensionality of preferences in voting in the UN General Assembly have found that it is "low-dimensional," in that one or at most two dimensions capture the majority of the variance in voting patterns (Russett and Kim 1996; Voeten 2000, 2004). Issues presented for consideration in multilateral security forums are often one dimensional, in that they involve "more pressure" to "less," or "intervention" to "sanctions." These options implicitly fall along a continuum from a more aggressive response to some international security situation to a less aggressive response or no response. It is important to note, however, that this approach ignores the bargaining and side payments that may occur between policy proposal and vote by the organization.

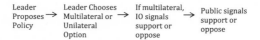

FIGURE 2.1   Game sequence

x, on the unidimensional line. The proposal is observed by everyone, but since policy implementation involves some unforeseen elements, the public does not know precisely where the policy outcome will fall. This captures the informational deficit faced by citizens; governments have access to more information that allows them to make an informed assessment of the likely consequences of their policies, while citizens know these consequences with much less precision. Additionally, assume the public knows its leader's and the pivotal member's ideal point with some error. In other words, citizens have some perceptions of the general predisposition of their own government, as well as that of other governments that vote in the multilateral institution, regarding efforts to overturn the status quo.

The basic game is illustrated in figure 2.1. In this initial setup, actors care only about policy and not about the potential consequences associated with that policy, such as the response of the international community.[15] Of course, in practice, these two concerns may be difficult to distinguish. I distinguish them here simply to isolate the dynamics of information transmission regarding policy. However, below I discuss how introducing a number of alternative concerns would affect the substantive conclusions.

I initially present a simple version of the game in which the pivotal member and public vote sincerely. This demonstrates the conditions under which the public can learn from the vote of the pivotal member. In subsequent sections I build more complexity into the sequence to analyze how the pivotal member should act and what the public can learn from the vote if the member rationally anticipates whether their vote can affect the leader's behavior.

PREFERENCES, BEHAVIOR, AND KNOWLEDGE

An appropriate equilibrium concept for this type of game is a perfect Bayesian equilibrium, which consists of a set of strategies that no player would rather deviate from and a set of beliefs (in this case, for the public) that are consistent with those strategies. Players begin the game with a set of prior

15. See Chapman 2007 for a slightly more complicated version of this game in which the pivotal member has an opportunity to impose a costly response that is felt by citizens.

beliefs about the state of nature—in this case, the true location of the eventual policy outcome, and update their beliefs according to Bayes's rule.

In this simple setup, I initially assume that players vote sincerely, in that they compare their utility under the status quo to their utility under the proposed policy. For the leader and pivotal member, this means a straightforward comparison of utility under the status quo versus a proposed policy choice. The public, however, compares their utility under the status quo to their expected utility for the policy. Since the public does not know the likely outcome of the policy they must calculate their utility given their expectation about the policy outcome. This expectation is based on prior beliefs, which are uninformed by third-party signals, and posterior beliefs, which are informed by the behavior of the leader and the pivotal member. The public's belief about likely policy outcomes is therefore a function of their leader's behavior—whether their leader proposes a policy and whether the leader chooses to consult a multilateral security institution—and the vote of the pivotal member.

However, the extent to which the public can learn from behavior depends upon their preferences relative to those of their leader and of the pivotal member. To illustrate this, consider a case in which the public holds policy preferences that fall farther from the status quo than both their leader and the pivotal member. In other words, the audience prefers policies that diverge very far from the status quo, while their leader and the pivotal member of the multilateral security institution hold more conservative preferences. Figure 2.2 represents this situation, with x_i^* representing the furthest policy from the status quo that actor i would be willing to support, and $i \in \{L, M, P\}$, for leader, pivotal member, and public.

In this situation, the leader will propose policy at x_L, its own ideal point, and the pivotal member and public always support the policy. The public knows that since all policies that fall within its leader's preferred policies also fall within its own, it prefers any policy its leader proposes to the status quo. However, such a scenario is not very interesting or realistic, if we are to believe a long line of political philosophy and empirical scholarship that suggests that citizens are usually more conservative in their foreign policy preferences than their leadership. If we accept that policies that diverge further from the status quo are generally more costly, then it is reasonable to analyze situations in which the public's preferences are more conservative than its leadership.[16]

---

16. Why would the public's foreign policy preferences diverge from those of its leader, particularly if that leader is elected? One answer is that elections occur in a multidimensional issue space, so that the

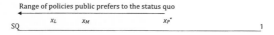

FIGURE 2.2   Hawkish public

Where should the pivotal members' preferences fall? In some cases, such as in the case of the UN Security Council, it is likely that for almost any state making a foreign policy proposal one member of the council will hold more conservative preferences. However, in other institutional settings it is possible that member states are perceived as willing to support nearly any proposal set forth by certain states. This appeared to be the case with the OAS during the cold war, as many perceived the organization to be dominated by the United States (Malone and Khong 2003; Slater 1969). This may also be the case in many instances in which the United States operated through NATO. Although NATO *members* have publicly opposed U.S. action in rare cases, such as the 2003 Iraq War, NATO as an organization has never openly and formally opposed a U.S. action. Both instances—those in which the pivotal member is more conservative than a proposing government and those in which the pivotal member is less conservative than a proposing government—represent interesting and plausible scenarios.

Finally, how should we conceive of the public's knowledge of its leader's and the pivotal member's foreign policy preferences? It may be a monumental assumption to assume that the public knows these preferences without error, if at all. However, in order for the public to update its beliefs about the likely policy outcome on the basis of the other actors' behavior, it must have some knowledge or perception of the incentives of its leadership and the pivotal member. In this game, those incentives come from policy preferences. However, we may relax the assumption of perfect information about policy preferences, and assume that the public only has an estimate of the pivotal member's preferences, represented by $\hat{x}_M = E[x_M + e]$, where $e \sim \theta(\mu, \sigma)$. In other words, the pivotal member's preferences are only known by the public with some error, due perhaps to unfamiliarity with foreign affairs or incentives to misrepresent foreign policy preferences on the part of foreign governments. The nature of this uncertainty is not a central focus of this model; rather, I include it to note that, consistent with existing empirical findings, the public may be poorly informed about foreign policy matters.

---

elected leader may not necessarily represent the median voter in every dimension. Another answer is that successive leaders may differ in resolve, which may differ from that of the public (cf. Wolford 2007).

An argument can be made that the public is more familiar with its leader's preferences than with foreign governments, as their leader reveals her preferences over time through statements and behavior. We can thus say that the public's estimate of their leaders preferences is $\hat{x}_L = E[x_L + r]$, where $r \sim \theta(\alpha, \gamma)$, and $\gamma < \sigma$. In other words, the possible variation around the leader's preferences is smaller than that around the pivotal member's. If this uncertainty is purely random and not systematic, the public's perception of their leader's preferences will converge to the true ideal point in expectation. If leaders systematically misrepresent their preferences in one particular direction, this may not be the case. I set aside this issue for the time being in order to focus on the informational properties of IO signals.

BELIEFS AND BEHAVIOR WITH A "CONSERVATIVE PIVOTAL MEMBER"

Consider the actors' behavior when the pivotal member prefers policies closer to the status quo than the audience or leader. If voting is costless and the pivotal member simply uses the multilateral forum to express her sincere preference, she will only support policies that fall within a narrow range of deviations from the status quo. Note that for any actor with an ideal point right of the status quo, any policy to the left of its ideal point but to the right of the status quo will be preferred to the status quo. Prior to observing the vote of the pivotal member, however, the public faces a dilemma. Their leader prefers a wide range of policies to the status quo, so simply observing that their leader has proposed a policy does not reveal to the public that the policy is one that they would prefer to support. This situation is illustrated in figure 2.3, where x_i^* represents the furthest policy from the status quo that actor i will support.

Upon seeing their leader propose some policy, the public is uncertain whether it falls in a range that it finds acceptable. The leader may propose a policy either unilaterally or multilaterally, but recall that leaders differ in the extent to which public opposition to foreign policy is costly. First, consider the case in which the leader is unconcerned about public opinion. This may the case in nondemocratic countries, or in cases in which the leader's ideal policy is so far from the status quo that it is willing to suffer a public backlash in order to revise the status quo. In such a case, the leader is indifferent as to whether the public or pivotal member will support the policy and it will simply propose its ideal point. The public and pivotal member may vote sincerely and oppose the policy, but this does not deter the leader, since

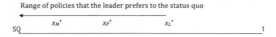

FIGURE 2.3   Dovish pivotal member (preferred leader policies)

neither actor can impose sufficient costs to prevent the leader from simply setting the policy proposal at her ideal point. In turn, the leader is indifferent between proposing the policy unilaterally or multilaterally. If the leader proposes the policy unilaterally the public cannot update its beliefs about the likely policy outcome; the public, observing a unilateral proposal, does not know whether the proposal would have passed the institution's voting procedure. Hence, the leader can simply propose her ideal point. However, if the leader offers a multilateral proposal, the public either updates that the policy is one it would like to support, in the case of multilateral support, or that it falls in a range between the pivotal member's preferred range and the leader's preferred range, in the case of multilateral opposition. In either case, the belief updating is quite tangential to the central behavior in the game, as the public's beliefs and behavior cannot affect the leader's behavior.

Second, consider the case in which the leader is attentive to public support, or the case in which public opposition is sufficiently costly, such that the leader will avoid proposing policies that will certainly invoke a public backlash. Here, the public's updated beliefs are central to determining the government's decision, because the public bases its decision on the information it can glean from the pivotal member's vote and the leader's decision. If the pivotal member supports a policy, the public updates that it is within its range of acceptable policies and will also support the policy.[17] However, if the pivotal member opposes a policy, the public is unable to determine whether or not it falls within the range of policies it prefers. It simply updates that the policy falls within the range between what the pivotal member prefers to the status quo and what their leader prefers to the status quo. This is illustrated in figure 2.4.

The public knows only that the policy is within the range that its leader prefers to the status quo (SQ to x_L^*) and outside of the range that the pivotal

17. This requires, however, that the error with which the public perceives the pivotal member's ideal point is not so large that the possible interval of the pivotal member's preferred policies falls outside of the public's.

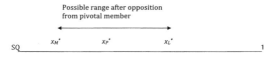

FIGURE 2.4   Dovish pivotal member (pivotal member opposition)

member prefers to the status quo (SQ to x_M^*). However, the public does not know whether the policy falls within the range it would prefer to the status quo (SQ to x_P^*), and thus makes its decision under uncertainty.

Under uncertainty, the public bases its decision on the likelihood that the pivotal member would oppose a policy that the public would support. This likelihood is determined by how conservative the pivotal member's preferences are relative to the public and its leader. As the pivotal member's range of acceptable alternatives to the status quo shrinks, it is more likely that it is vetoing a policy that the public actually would prefer, were it to know the likely outcome. However, as the range of alternatives that the pivotal member prefers to the status quo moves right or expands, the likelihood of it vetoing a policy that the public prefers decreases.

What does this imply for the leader? A leader who prefers public support should always consult an institution that she expects to support her policy, as support from an institution with a pivotal member who is more conservative than the public will guarantee public support. In turn, should a leader who wants public support choose unilateralism, the public should infer that the pivotal member would have voted against the proposal. Therefore, upon seeing a unilateral proposal from a public opinion–conscious leader, the public should hold the same beliefs as it would upon seeing opposition from the pivotal member—that the likely outcome falls somewhere between what the pivotal member finds acceptable and what their leader finds acceptable. This means that the leader should be indifferent between consulting the institution and making a unilateral proposal—the public, the actor it primarily cares about, learns the same thing when opposition is expected.

Due to the logic of belief updating, from the leader's point of view, a conservative institution offers a large public opinion benefit if it offers its support. Importantly, opposition from a conservative institution does not automatically engender public opposition, particularly if that institution is perceived as very conservative, or having a very small range of policies it prefers to the status quo. This creates strong incentives for a leader to consult more conservative institutions. This logic leads to several hypotheses about behavior.

Hypothesis 1: Public support for foreign policies is likely to increase with multilateral support and as the multilateral institution is perceived as more conservative, or more ideologically distant from the state proposing the policy.

Hypothesis 1 follows from how the public updates its beliefs upon observing institutional support. As the institution is seen as more distant from the proposing actor and as holding a status quo bias, the public is more likely to take support as indicative that the policy falls within their preferred range. In other words, the public believes that the policy will not be overly costly or aggressive and should be supported.

Hypothesis 2: Public support for foreign policies is less likely to be affected by multilateral opposition as the multilateral institution is perceived as more conservative, or more ideologically distant from the proposing state.

Hypothesis 2 follows from how the public updates its beliefs upon observing institutional opposition. Opposition from a conservative actor could mean that the policy is not one that the public prefers, or it could simply mean that the pivotal member has a very different set of foreign policy preferences than the public. However, as the pivotal member's range of acceptable alternatives to the status quo increases, the public is more likely to believe that the pivotal member's response indicates that the policy is undesirable (from their point of view) and will oppose it.

Hypothesis 3: Leaders who desire public support for policies face greater incentives to consult multilateral institutions as those institutions become more conservative.

Hypothesis 3 is derived from the logic of the leader's decision. Support from institutions that are perceived to be more conservative by the public will guarantee public support, while opposition is less likely to engender public opposition. In a probabilistic world, the so-called risk-reward trade-off facing leaders becomes more favorable as a multilateral institution becomes more conservative. Of course, at the extreme, conservative institutions may not support any policy a leader proposes, in which case the leader may find it not worthwhile to even consult the institution, particularly if doing so is costly in terms of delay (cf. Brooks and Wohlforth 2005). However, the general logic holds that leaders face greater incentives to consult the institution as it is *perceived* by the public to be more conservative.

As an illustrative example, this logic helps explain both the boost in approval for the first Gulf War following the November 1990 Security Council resolution, and the lack of a public backlash for failing to obtain Security Council approval prior to the 2003 Iraq War. I discuss these cases in more detail in chapter 4, but it is useful to briefly consider the public reactions to UN Security Council activity surrounding these two events. In both cases, the U.S. public expressed strong preferences for UN Security Council sanction prior to taking any military action. In the former case, the UN Security Council resolution in November 1990 appeared to boost at least short-term support for the war (see Mueller 1994, 32). In the latter case, the United States of course did not receive Security Council authorization, but support for the war in initial months was high and President George W. Bush received a thirteen-point spike in approval ratings immediately after the onset of the war in March 2003. If the public views the Security Council as conservative in granting authorization for war, the model would suggest precisely these empirical patterns. Support from the conservative UN Security Council would greatly increase public support for war, while opposition may do little to dampen public support.

These claims are consistent with Thompson (2006), who locates the UN Security Council's ability to communicate benign intent in its neutrality. Where the observer's, or public's, preferences perfectly conform with those of the pivotal member, signals from the pivotal member are perfectly informative about whether the policy falls within or outside of the range the public supports. However, this assumption may not be realistic in the context of multilateral security institutions, as voting members often have direct stakes in the outcome of events. This has important implications for the informational content of IO decisions.

BELIEFS AND BEHAVIOR WITH AN "EXPANSIONIST PIVOTAL MEMBER"

Another possible preference ordering is one in which the pivotal member's range of acceptable alternatives to the status quo is larger than that of the public. This might be the perception if a particular organization is seen as "captured" by a particularly powerful state or comprised of members with very similar interests to a proposing state. First, consider the case in which the member's preferences are actually more expansive than the leader, illustrated in figure 2.5. In this instance, support from the pivotal member does not provide the public with any additional information about the likely policy outcome beyond what they know from observing their leader pro-

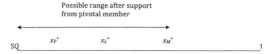

FIGURE 2.5   Hawkish pivotal member (pivotal member support)

pose the policy. Recall that leaders will only propose policies that fall within their range of acceptable alternatives (SQ to x_L^*). Since this range falls within the range of the pivotal member's acceptable alternatives, it does not signal anything new to the public.[18]

Consider the case, however, in which the pivotal member is more conservative than the public but less so than the leader, illustrated in figure 2.6. In this case, the public can truncate the range of possible policy outcomes upon seeing support from the pivotal member, although it cannot conclude with certainty that the likely outcome falls within the range it prefers to the status quo (SQ to x_P^*). However, because it can truncate its range of beliefs, there is a greater chance that the public will support a policy that receives support from a more aggressive or expansive pivotal member. This chance increases as the pivotal member's preferences become more conservative, or as they come closer to coinciding with those of the public. On the other hand, opposition from a more expansive pivotal member will tend to provoke public opposition, as the public can update that the likely outcome will fall far from its range of acceptable alternatives to the status quo. Therefore, opposition from such an institution can have a strong affect on public attitudes.

What does this imply for the leader's behavior? Again, to the extent that support will increase the chances of public support, leaders face an incentive to consult such institutions whenever they anticipate being able to garner support. However, opposition from such an institution can be very costly to public opinion conscious leaders. Unlike opposition from a more conservative institution, which may not immediately result in public opposition, opposition from a more expansive or revisionist institution will likely cause public opposition because it is expected to support almost any reasonable policy. This leads to three additional empirical implications.

18. In the off-equilibrium-path event that the leader proposes a policy that the pivotal member opposes, it is unclear what the public should conclude. A candidate belief is that the public updates its beliefs in order to minimize the chance of supporting a policy outside its preferred range, and concludes that opposition indicates that the policy is outside of its preferred range. Another candidate is that it simply retains its priors, in which case it would calculate an expected utility for the policy and compare it to its utility for the status quo.

FIGURE 2.6   Moderate pivotal member

Hypothesis 4: Public support for foreign policies is likely to increase with multilateral support and as the multilateral institution is perceived as more conservative, but this effect is diminished if institutions are perceived as more likely than the public to support a given foreign policy initiative.

Hypothesis 4 points out that compared to the previous preference ordering, support from a more revisionist institution, while *improving* the chances of public support, does not automatically do so. The effect of support from an institution that is perceived *ex ante* to be willing to support most policies the leader might propose is less effective at boosting public support than an institution that is seen as very conservative with its sanction.

Hypothesis 5: Public support for foreign policies is likely to decrease with multilateral opposition and as the multilateral institution is perceived as more revisionist.

Hypothesis 5 is derived from what the public should believe upon seeing a more revisionist institution reject their leader's policies. Rejection suggests that the public also would not care to support to support the policy if they knew its likely outcome.

Hypothesis 6: Leaders who desire public support for policies face greater incentives to consult revisionist or expansive multilateral institutions as those institutions become more conservative relative to their citizens.

Hypothesis 7: Leaders who desire public support for policies should avoid the disapproval of revisionist institutions.

Hypotheses 6 and 7 suggest that although the effect of support from a more revisionist institution may be second best to the support of a more conservative institution, in terms of providing a public opinion boost, it is still preferable to no support. On the other hand, leaders should actively avoid the disapproval of institutions that are seen as more revisionist or *ex ante* likely to support their policies. This may be one reason states seek policies that can garner the support of traditional allies; although these allies are expected to support their policies, opposition raises questions about the wisdom of the policy. On the other hand, consistent with the logic laid out in the previous section, leaders may attempt to paint former allies that oppose them as overly conservative or unreasonable in their position in order to avoid opposition as being seen as signaling information about the merits of their proposed policy.

As an example, consider U.S. policy surrounding the 1983 invasion of Grenada. The United States did not approach the UN Security Council in this case, as the cold war stance of Russia often precluded consensus amongst the P-5, especially on the issue of Communist influence in the Caribbean, and China's posture normally opposed such interventions in sovereign countries. However, the United States did approach the Organization of American States, which did not support the invasion, and ultimately turned to the Organization of Eastern Caribbean States, which granted authorization for the invasion. The sanction of the OECS had little effect on public support for the invasion, in the United States, however, which was already high (cf. Eichenberg 2005).[19] If the public believed that the OECS was subject to U.S. domination or manipulation, as an organization comprised of small states under direct U.S. geographic and economic influence, the model would predict exactly this lack of effect. In other words, when an organization that is *ex ante* expected to grant support offers its support, it should have little effect on public attitudes toward the policy at hand.

BEHAVIOR IN THE SHADOW OF IMPLEMENTATION

The scenarios presented thus far say very little about how actors should behave if they anticipate whether their votes or support will actually affect policy implementation or other outcomes in the future. For instance, should the pivotal member veto a policy that it fully expects to be implemented? Should the public oppose its leadership if the leadership intends to implement a policy with or without public support?

These questions can be answered by adding an implementation stage to the

---

19. The Reagan administration went to some length to build a case for intervention, using the request from the OECS for U.S. military intervention as potential legal justification. However, the immediate public response was mixed and the media questioned the meaning of OECS authorization (Western 2005, 128).

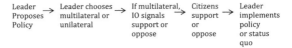

FIGURE 2.7   Game sequence with implementation

game, illustrated in figure 2.7, such that after the public makes its decision, the leader must decide whether to back down or implement the policy. Suppose that the public can only impose a political cost on its leader if the leader follows through and implements her policy after the public opposes it. Suppose also that there are two types of leaders—those for whom public opposition is prohibitively costly and those for whom public opposition does not affect the implementation decision. In reality, this may depend on how close the likely outcome of the policy is to the leader's preferred preferences; when the leader can implement a policy very close or identical to her preferred policy she may be willing tolerate more public opposition, and vice versa.

The tolerance of leaders for public opposition is important because it determines the extent to which the public can constrain the leadership and, by extension, the degree to which the pivotal member can indirectly affect policy implementation. When leaders are not attentive to public opinion, neither the public nor the pivotal member can influence outcomes. Thus, if we no longer assume simple sincere voting and allow voting to be influenced by the anticipation of whether it can affect the outcome, there is an equilibrium to this game in which the pivotal member and the public are completely indifferent about supporting or opposing policy, *even if it falls far from their preferred range*, because their behavior cannot affect implementation. We might call this a "babbling equilibrium," in the sense that multilateral support and opposition are both possible and the public cannot deduce whether the pivotal member's decision is based on policy preferences and therefore cannot glean policy-relevant information from the signal.

However, public and media support is often critical for foreign policy success.[20] If the leader relies on public support for implementation and the pivotal member can affect public beliefs and therefore public support, the pivotal member and public again can vote on the basis of whether they prefer the status quo to the proposed policy. Thus, the degree to which institutions can be influential through providing policy-relevant information

20. Pevehouse and Howell 2007; Baum 2003.

depends on the degree to which leaders, who are ultimately responsible for implementing policy, are concerned about public support.

Hypothesis 8: The influence of institutional decisions should be strongest for democracies and in cases in which leaders are likely to be highly attentive to public opinion.

Hypothesis 8 flows from the notion that the costliness of public opposition to foreign policy varies across countries and situations as a function of domestic institutions and contemporary factors that might affect public support for a leader, such as economic conditions.

One final implication of incorporating domestic constraints into the considerations of the leader is that the need to acquire public approval may often provoke policy moderation. To see this, imagine a scenario in which a leader will only implement a proposed policy if they are confident that it will enjoy broad public support. Furthermore, suppose that the public is unlikely to support the proposal unless it acquires multilateral support. The leader, therefore, is placed in the difficult position of proposing a policy that can gain international organization support. However, since that support is only forthcoming if the proposed policy falls within an acceptable range to the pivotal member, the leader must deviate from proposing a more extreme policy in order to acquire organizational authorization.

In the less extreme case that the public may discount some opposition, meaning that authorization is not vital to obtaining public support, the leader must still moderate her publicly announced proposal to assuage public concerns. In other words, because of uncertainty about policy consequences, a relatively hawkish leader must moderate demands in order to garner public support. This incentive is stronger when the public relies on cues from a multilateral organization. We should then observe more policy moderation and compromise in a world with a multilateral organization that makes public pronouncements on foreign policy than a world without such an institution.

STRATEGIC AND SINCERE VOTING

To this point the actors under consideration have had a relatively simple set of incentives. Specifically, actors evaluate proposed policies relative to the existing status quo and perhaps care about whether their behavior may ultimately affect the implementation of proposed policies. It is worth discussing, however, other possible sources of incentives. I relegate these factors to a less formal discussion because I focus primarily on relative preferences in subsequent chapters, although I incorporate concerns over some of the following factors in empirical tests.

PUBLIC CONCERN ABOUT MULTILATERAL OPPOSITION

If the public is ultimately concerned about the costliness of a policy, they may be attentive to whether the member states of an institution will ultimately impose costs beyond simply voicing their opposition with a veto. Moreover, they may also be concerned about whether multilateral opposition will translate into material opposition from other states in the system. For instance, it is likely that the failure to obtain UN Security Council authorization for the 2003 Iraq War influenced Turkey's decision to refuse basing rights to the United States. However, if the public is uncertain about member states' preferences it also follows that they may be uncertain about the likelihood or costliness of subsequent material opposition. In some cases, such as a threatened Russian veto of the 1999 Kosovo operation, opposition may be viewed as more symbolic than as a real threat to implement costly obstruction. Thus, if we were to introduce the public's concern about the potential costs of multilateral opposition we could complicate the public's expected utility calculation by including uncertainty about the costliness of an operation upon seeing opposition. In some cases, particularly in cases in which great powers' vetoes are very salient and convey some real threat, the public's estimate of the probable costliness of a course of action may be large enough to deter their support, even if they strictly prefer the likely policy outcome to the status quo. Again, however, this relies on the specificity of public knowledge of foreign states preferences and resolve, which is likely only known with some error.

The introduction of this factor would allow the model to speak to how public anticipation of multilateral responses to foreign policies might be affected by institutional decisions. This is a central claim of Voeten's explanation of the UN Security Council's ability to legitimate the use of force (2005). However, Voeten's argument does not include the possibility that the public's anticipation of such costs may be quite variable and subject to their perceptions of states' preferences and resolve. The possibility that citizens are uncertain about potential multilateral responses and look to institutional decisions in order to develop better estimates about the costliness of foreign policy again implies more variance in responses to institutional institutions than is commonly suggested. These expectations are tied to the relative preferences of member states, in that member states are more likely to attempt to raise the costs of unilateralism when policies are implemented that are far outside their range of acceptable policies.

COMMITMENT, AUDIENCE COSTS, AND REPUTATION

A large amount of scholarship since Fearon's seminal piece on audience costs (1994) suggests that leaders face negative political consequences for backing down from threats during crises. Recently, Tomz (2007b) found empirical support for this notion in an experiment with a sample of U.S. citizens, although Schultz (2001b) noted the difficulty of directly observing these costs due to selection effects. Proposing policies publicly through a multilateral forum may invoke similar costs, in the sense that it commits governments to following through with their proposals.[21] If governments pay a substantial cost for backing down from their multilateral proposals, it likely means that the policy would enjoy widespread support. Again, this would reduce the pivotal member's influence because her vote would not affect implementation. In such a case, the pivotal member should simply be indifferent about her vote. She may vote sincerely to make a symbolic point (or because she is attentive to other political concerns, discussed below), but she cannot affect outcomes. In practice, states often voice their displeasure with various foreign policies because of other concerns, such as signaling to a domestic audience or to maintain their reputation. The main point is that channeling foreign policy through a multilateral institution may lock states into certain foreign policy directions because of the desire to avoid looking weak to domestic audiences. Institutions can serve as an international stage for costly position taking and publicize states' positions more so than unilateral proclamations. In such an environment, it may be difficult for the institution's voting members to dissuade aggressive states from backing down, but the process of holding multilateral debate raises global awareness and puts the proposing state's initiatives in the spotlight.

A second concern relates to the value of reputation to the state (cf. Sartori 2005). Governments may be attentive to the diplomatic reputation they earn in order to preserve their ability to communicate in future crises. Although the exact nature of reputation formation is debated (e.g., Mercer 1996; Hopf 1994; Guisinger and Smith 2002), rationalist scholars would maintain that failing to follow through on threats may make diplomacy more difficult to conduct in the future or may create a reputation of weakness. Reputation costs

21. See also Leventoglu and Tarar 2005.

may, in some instances, offset the political costs of implementing unpopular policies, which would again render public opinion and the pivotal member's decision impotent in terms of changing outcomes. In these cases we would also expect the pivotal member and public to be indifferent, as they cannot affect outcomes, unless they are concerned about the symbolic benefits of opposition or if the pivotal member herself has other political incentives to voice opposition, which I turn to next. Thus, reputational costs and public commitment may produce outcomes in which leaders are unwilling to back down even from policies that will not receive multilateral support.

MEMBER STATE POLITICS AND ISSUE LINKAGE

Two additional sources of incentives for member states of an institution are worth noting. First, member states (or the pivotal member in the model) may have their own domestic political reasons for voting a certain way. For instance, antiwar public opinion in France likely played at least some role in the French threat to veto a resolution authorizing invasion in 2003. Second, states may be concerned about issue linkage and side payments. For instance, China chose to abstain from the 1994 vote authorizing the Haiti invasion, likely due to U.S. concessions on its accession to the WTO. These two possibilities raise interesting questions about the informational content of member state decisions.

What should an observer who is seeking policy-relevant information conclude from a vote that is possibly the product of political side deals? In practice, much of this compromising and negotiation takes place behind closed doors and ordinary citizens would not by privy to such information (Prantl 2005), but the possibility that the vote reflects concerns other than the issue at hand raises questions about the policy relevance of the information conveyed by the vote. Similarly, if the vote happens to be driven more by political concerns among a member state's home constituency, the policy relevance of the vote is brought into question. Since citizens are unlikely to know the details of such considerations, these concerns may play a role only in extreme cases or when the media actively highlights the public opposition to a policy among a member state's domestic population. Nonetheless, the possibility of voting being driven by concerns other than policy preferences may affect the belief updating of observers.

One possibility is that vetoes may carry little weight, even if the member state is a traditional ally, if the veto is perceived as driven by non–policy-relevant considerations, such as pleasing a domestic constituency. This may have been the case with regard to the publicly threatened French veto in

2003. Support in the face of potential domestic disagreement, on the other hand, may strengthen the credibility or legitimacy of authorization. A possible instance of this dynamic is the 1991 Persian Gulf War, which received the support of many Arab countries in the Middle East. At the same time, support may be down-weighted if the public knows that it was made possible by "vote buying," such as may have been the case when China abstained from the Haiti vote. These scenarios highlight the need to consider concerns beyond policy merits when studying empirical events.

It is worth noting that the actual role of the *organization* in this theoretical analysis could be seen as quite limited, beyond simply providing a forum for the expression of member state preferences. This is because the theoretical model is designed consciously to make no assumptions about the ability of the organization itself to behave independently of the member states for two core reasons. First, one alternative hypotheses against which this book's evidence should be assessed is the realist claim that organizational "talk" does not influence state behavior. To the extent that the organization is doing little here but providing a voice or forum for member states to take issues and vote on formal statements, this setup provides a "hard case" for comparison to realist claims that multilateral security IOs are essentially relevant, while admitting the basic realist principle that states tend to drive IO decisions. To the extent that the IO is powerless in this model to enforce its mandates, the model incorporates realist assumptions but yields different conclusions.

The second main alternative hypothesis that this book addresses is the claim that citizens prefer multilateralism because it is "procedurally correct," suggesting that consulting an IO should nearly always result in larger boosts in public support of leaders and be a preferred strategy of leaders, or that certain IOs are legitimate, suggesting that their authorization should always result in larger boosts in public support. The model presented here suggests an alternative process, driven by state preferences and not by assumptions about IO agency.

While a number of scholars have claimed that IOs provide legitimacy for security policies, the consequences of distributive conflicts within institutions have not been properly addressed. In particular, institutional decisions tend to reflect the preferences of member states, raising questions about why audiences regard decisions as legitimate, or when audiences will update their beliefs about a policy in a manner that causes them to support policies. In turn, if it is beneficial for leaders to consult institutions in order to garner public support, it is unclear when leaders will deem it favorable to do so. In this chapter I presented a model of strategic information transmission that demonstrates audiences will tend to act in accordance with institutional decisions when decisions contradict the perceived biases of member states. When institutional decisions appear to reinforce these biases, decisions may be discounted, depending on the relationship between the preferences of the audience, those of its leader, and those of the institution. The credibility of institutional signals of opposition is also critical to whether decisions are ignored. This credibility can be affected by international and domestic costs, which implies that the political situations of member states can influence how institutional decisions will be received.

These results shed new light on several areas of interest in international relations scholarship. First, the theory predicts that leaders are more likely to consult international institutions that disagree with them about policy, particularly if those leaders depend on public support for policy implementation. On the other hand, when institutions are more likely to offer support, leaders will be careful to avoid their disapproval. Second, domestic audiences should be more likely to support policies that receive authorization from conservative institutions. Anecdotal public opinion data and scattered evidence appear to support this conjecture, but it should be subjected to further testing. Finally, the model suggests that there is a trade-off between designing an institution capable of conferring legitimacy through its support and an institution capable of deterring policymakers from proposing expansive foreign policies due to anticipation of the ill effects of opposition on public opinion. While conservative institutions are able to provide confidence to the public with authorization, revisionist institutions may be better equipped to constrain policymakers, as their opposition may induce public opposition.

Why do statements issued by institutions carry additional weight beyond those of individual countries? First, institutions can serve as public forums that focus greater attention on policy-relevant statements than would ordinarily be devoted to the ad hoc statements of individual countries. Second, institutions can make public position taking more costly for states, causing observers to attribute greater significance to institutional decisions over the individual statements of states. Third, the symbolic importance of a formal institution may increase the attention paid its decisions, while observers may still able to distinguish the possible motivations members driving those decisions. Within this framework, then, we should expect the effect of institutional decisions on public attitudes at home and abroad to be conditional on perceptions of member states interests.

APPENDIX: FORMAL DISCUSSION OF MODEL AND EQUILIBRIA

I begin by discussing utility calculations in the initial simple model with no implementation and sincere voting and build on that logic to describe behavior when actors can anticipate implementation. To maintain accessibility, this appendix focuses on sketching the logic of a proof in mostly prose rather than mathematics.

SINCERE VOTING

Under the sincere voting assumption, the pivotal member compares her utility for the policy, x, to her utility under the status quo, o. The pivotal member votes in support of the policy when

$$-(x - x_M)^2 \geq -(0 - x_M)^2$$
$$x \geq 2x_M$$

The leader proposes only policies that she prefers to the status quo, such that

$$-(x - x_L)^2 \geq -(0 - x_L)^2$$
$$x \geq 2x_L$$

These critical values correspond to $x_M{}^*$ and $x_L{}^*$ in this chapter. The public would like to support policies that it sincerely prefers to the status quo, but is uncertain about the policy outcome, x, and the exact location of the pivotal member's ideal point, x_M. For simplicity assume the public's prior beliefs about the location of $x \sim U[0,1]$ and that the public's prior beliefs about the location of $x_M = E[x_M + e]$.

Upon observing the leader propose a policy, x, the public updates its beliefs according to Bayes's rule and concludes that $x \in [x, 2x_L]$. First consider the case of a "conservative" pivotal member, such that $x_P < x_M < x_L$. When this is the case, the public can update its beliefs again upon seeing a signal of either support or opposition. When the pivotal member signals support, the public updates that $x \leq E[x_M + e]$. If e is so large that $E[x_M + e] > x_L$, the signal of support is *uninformative*, as it does not allow the public to update beliefs beyond what it already could conclude from observing its leader propose a policy. At the other extreme, if $E[x_M + e] \leq 2x_P$, the signal of support is *fully revealing*, as it clearly demonstrates to the public that the policy is within the range it would prefer to the status quo.

We can thus say that when $x_M < x_P$ and e is sufficiently small— ($E[x_M + e] \leq 2x_P$)—there exists a fully revealing perfect Bayesian equilibrium in which the policymaker proposes x, the pivotal member issues her support, and the public updates with certainty that the policy is one it would like to support.

Likewise, when $x_M > x_P$, or the pivotal member has an ideal point further from the status quo of the public, a signal of opposition from the pivotal member is fully revealing, provided e is not negative and so large that $E[x_M + e] < 2x_P$. In this instance, there exists a fully revealing perfect Bayesian equilibrium in which the leader proposes the policy, the pivotal member signals opposition, and the public updates with certainty that the policy is not one that they would like to support.

When a conservative pivotal member opposes a policy proposal or a more revisionist pivotal member supports a policy proposal, the signal is only *partially revealing*, in that it allows the public to partially update its beliefs, but not conclude with certainty whether or not the policy falls within or outside the range it prefers to the status quo. The public's updated beliefs are calculated according to the voting thresholds established for sincere voting, such that upon opposition from conservative pivotal the audience beliefs x is such that $2E[x_M + e] < x < 2x_L$. The public's compares its expected utility for support to the status quo:

$$\int_{2E[x_M+e]}^{2x_L} -(x - x_P)^2 U dx \geq -(0 - x_P)^2$$

The public will support the policy if $x < x_P{}^*$, where $x_P{}^* \equiv F(x_P, x_L, x_M, e)$, and $\dfrac{\partial x_P^*}{\partial x_L} < 0$, $\dfrac{\partial x_P^*}{\partial x_M} > 0$, $\dfrac{\partial x_P^*}{\partial x_P} > 0$. Opposition from a conservative member does not automatically induce opposition from the public, particularly if the public's preferences are closer to its leadership and further away from the pivotal member and if the error surrounding the public's estimate of the pivotal member's preferences is small.

Support from a more revisionist institution yields an updated belief that

$x < \mathrm{E}[x_M + e]$. The public then compares its expected utility for support to its utility under the status quo:

$$\int_0^{2E[x_M+e]} -(x - x_P)^2 U dx \geq -(0 - x_P)^2$$

The public will again support the policy if $x < x_P^*$, $x_P^* \equiv \mathrm{F}(x_M, e, x_P)$, $\dfrac{\partial x_P^*}{\partial x_M} > 0$, $\dfrac{\partial x_P^*}{\partial x_P} > 0$. Support from a revisionist member does not automatically induce public support, but is more likely to do so if the member's preferences conform closer to the audiences (or move more conservative) and if the error surrounding the public's estimation of the pivotal member's preferences is small.

How should the leader select the policy proposal? Suppose leaders compare their utility of a proposal, x, that garners public support to an alternative, x', that engenders public opposition: $-(x - x_L)^2 \geq -(x' - x_L)^2 - c$, where c is the cost of public opposition. In the unilateral case, when the public infers that there would not have been IO support, and when $c < (x - x_L)(x + x' - 2x_L)$, the leader will simply propose her ideal point, as leader is willing to incur public disapproval. When $c > (x - x_L)(x + x' - 2x_L)$, the leader will propose a policy that can gain public support. The optimal policy that can gain public support falls at the boundary of the public's range of acceptable policies, or x_P^*.

VOTING IN THE SHADOW OF IMPLEMENTATION

Once the implementation move is introduced, the audience and the pivotal member vote anticipating whether or not they can affect the policy outcome that occurs. This is conditional on the cost the leadership incurs for implementing policy that is unpopular with the public. Let $c > 0$ represent this cost. We can assume that leaders have different costs, or c's, in practice, although the leader in the current model has a fixed cost owing to the nature of political institutions or the present popularity of that leader. The leader now must compare her utility under implementation versus the status quo, *conditional* on the public's decision of support oppose. If the public supports, the comparison is the same as above, under sincere voting. If the public opposes the leader pays γ for implementing the policy, such that she only implements the policy if

$$c < x(2x_L - x)$$

Thus, c must be sufficiently small before the leader will implement politically unpopular policies. If this is the case, the public cannot influence the leader and the pivotal member cannot indirectly influence the leader; in other words the policy will be implemented regardless. In this situation, a babbling equilibrium results, as the public and pivotal member are each indifferent regarding support opposition and may do either.

However, when c is sufficiently large, the public can induce implementation with its support and deter implementation with its opposition. This reduces to a choice between utility under the policy and utility under the status quo, as the utility calculations under sincere voting describe. The leader, for her part, has complete information and will avoid implementing policies that the public opposes. Since the leader can anticipate public opposition based on knowledge of the public and how it will update its beliefs based on institutional signals, it will avoid proposing policies that will receive public opposition.

EXISTENCE OF BABBLING EQUILIBRIUM

Since the pivotal member's signal is costless—that is, the sender does not incur a penalty for lying—there are, of course, a number of possible babbling equilibria to this game in which the pivotal member's signal is not conditional on the true location of x. I focus above on fully and partially revealing equilibria, since these are of the most substantive interest. Also, if the pivotal member intends to affect outcomes, it has a strategic incentive to attempt to influence citizens in its preferred direction.

OUT OF EQUILIBRIUM BELIEFS

The assumption of sincere voting allows us to nicely examine belief updating when voting signals or judgments are believed to convey information about true preferences, but this updating relies on an implicit notion of what citizens would believe should actors choose signals that are not sincere. One candidate assumption is that citizens will always update as if they believe signals are sincere, which would create the incentive for member states to send signals that will produce behavior in line with their preferences. For example, if citizens would respond to an opposition signal from a conservative pivotal member with corresponding opposition to a proposed policy that is, in fact, one that falls within the member's acceptable range of policies, then the member has no incentive to deviate to this off-equilibrium path and produce this less desirable outcome.

Suppose citizens were unwilling to subscribe to such a "trusting" off-equilibrium path belief and instead never updated their beliefs in response to off-equilibrium path signals (it is not clear why this would be the case if they do update on the equilibrium path but consider it for the sake of argument). In this case, again, member states would not be able to influence public beliefs with their signals and hence lose their ability to influence outcomes toward those they find more desirable (by making the public less likely to support policies they oppose and more likely to support policies they like).

3

APPEALING TO MULTILATERAL SECURITY ORGANIZATIONS

It is now quite common for states to seek external approval when conducting foreign policy (Voeten 2005; Thompson 2006). Why states should consult multilateral institutions when considering policies designed to defend or further their self-interest is perplexing, however, given that these organizations typically lack the capacity to punish those who act *without* their approval. In chapter 2 I put forth an argument explaining how the decisions of these institutions can, under certain conditions, convey important information about possible foreign policy outcomes to less informed audiences, including domestic and foreign publics. One way leaders can gain the support of these publics is to gain the authorization of a multilateral security institution, like the UN Security Council.

In general, scholars posit that obtaining approval is important for four interrelated reasons. First, the sanction of large, multilateral institutions can signal that important states in the international system do not regard a foreign policy as overly aggressive (Voeten 2005). This is beneficial, as it means that key states in the international system are unlikely to obstruct the policy, therefore the costs of the policy are lowered and the likelihood of success is improved. Second, the sanction of a multilateral institution may free up domestic constraints in foreign countries (Thompson 2006). Third, the approval of institutions like the UNSC may help facilitate coordination and foreign policy success, at both the strategic and tactical levels (Martin

1992; Drezner 2000; Fearon and Laitin 2004). This may occur because the institution makes partners more likely to honor foreign policy commitments (Martin 1992) or because the legitimization of the institution loosens domestic constraints for potential allies (Thompson 2006). Finally, the support of IOs may provide domestic benefits for the state proposing a foreign policy, in essence alleviating domestic concerns about whether a proposed action is "appropriate" or worth the costs (Chapman and Reiter 2004; Chapman 2007; Fang 2008; Chapman 2009).

These mechanisms depend, in large part, on the ability of an institution to credibly signal information to external audiences. However, there is at least anecdotal evidence that ability of IOs to credibly signal information may vary across institutions and foreign policy contexts and according to what observers believe about the organization in question. For example, the Iraq War of 2003 was widely regarded internationally as illegitimate due to the opposition of key members of the UNSC (Mitzen 2005; Rubin 2003), while it was apparently regarded as legitimate by large segments of the U.S. population, according to public opinion polls (Eichenberg 2005; see also Chapman and Reiter 2004; Grieco 2003). The U.S. intervention in Kosovo was widely regarded as legitimate internationally, while domestic audiences in the U.S. expressed some trepidation that the campaign had not been endorsed by the UNSC (Johnstone 2004; Mitzen 2005; Voeten 2005; Chapman and Reiter 2004). In the former case, the U.S. public discounted UN Security Council opposition. In the latter case, some foreign audiences discounted NATO support. Given this variation in deference to international institutions, it is unclear when leaders will view the authorization of an IO as "beneficial enough" to invest time and resources into seeking a supportive or authorizing resolution. Leaders clearly choose when to consult multilateral organizations and which organizations to consult.

The theory in chapter 2 provides one account of when authorization will be worth seeking. Specifically, the reaction of audiences to the decisions of an IO depends on the foreign policy preferences of member states within the relevant institution. When the institution issues a decision that appears to contradict the preferences of member states, audiences will tend to regard decisions as more credible signals about the merits of a proposed policy. For instance, when a state with very different foreign policy preferences than a state proposing a given policy decides to consent to the policy, it sends a very strong signal to external audiences that the proposed policy is one worth supporting. This explains why authorization from the Security Council is so coveted—it is difficult to achieve consensus among the P-5. When an institution issues a decision that reinforces the known preferences of member states, audiences are able to conclude less about the merits of the proposed policy. From the point of view of many international observers, this seemed to be the case in the Kosovo example above, in that NATO supported a U.S. initiative. This also helps explain why Security Council opposition (or oppositional statements from key members) prior to the 2003 Iraq War did not dissuade many U.S. citizens from supporting the war.

This logic implies that leaders face an interesting trade-off when attempting to garner authorization from an IO. One the one hand, if an IO is perceived to be relatively conservative with its support of foreign policy ventures, its support is very beneficial for making a public case for the merits of an initiative while opposition will often be discounted. However, if the members of an IO are perceived to be friendly to the proposing state's interests and the IO issues a negative ruling, audiences are much more likely to oppose the policy. Thus, leaders have a strong incentive to consult institutions whose members are ex ante *unlikely* to rubber stamp their policies, as the risk-reward trade-off (a signal that is discounted by audiences versus a strong signal of legitimacy) is favorable from their perspective.

This chapter develops the first test of this logic on the decisions of states to consult global and regional security organizations during crises. I first discuss several cases in which leaders have commonly sought IO approval for domestic reasons. Second, I briefly review an alternative, normative explanation for why leaders might appeal to IOs during international crises. I then use the informational logic to motivate hypotheses about the domestic and international incentives for leaders to obtain the sanction of international institutions.

Notably, I argued in chapters 1 and 2 that the domestic benefits of obtaining IO approval are important. This means that domestic institutions and political conditions can create incentives for leaders to appeal to the international security organizations. Securing approval is particularly important for leaders of democracies who rely on public support for foreign policies. This incentive may be heightened during times in which public approval for a leader is low, like during declining economic conditions. The need for external approval may also be more acute for foreign policy actions that pose a substantial risk of casualties for the population.[1] During these times public support for foreign policy and for the leader is less certain, which provides leaders with a reason to obtain the support of an external source. In the remainder of the chapter I develop these arguments in more detail and

1. See Gartner 2008; Gartner and Segura 1998; and Gelpi, Feaver, and Reifler 2005–2006.

present empirical tests of the decision to appeal to security organizations during international crises.

International relations scholars have offered a variety of explanations for why leaders might work though international organizations. Institutions can facilitate agreements through providing information during bargaining (Boehmer, Gartzke, and Nordstrom 2004) or by serving as coordination devices (Martin 1992; Drezner 2000), reducing transaction costs and improving the chances of policy success (Abbott and Snidal 1998). The model presented in chapter 2 offers a distinct informational explanation for why leaders consult international institutions. While previous work suggests that leaders generally act as if it is important to garner multilateral authorization (Voeten 2005), the ideas presented here suggest that it is not always equally important to do so. Leaders who desire public support are more likely to consult international institutions as the "risk-reward" trade-off of consultation becomes more favorable or as institutions become more conservative.

The favorable risk-return trade-off of consulting conservative institutions arises because getting approval increases the chances of public support while opposition does not carry the automatic sanction that comes with opposition from more revisionist institutions. For instance, the argument in chapter 2 explains both the decision to bring the Iraq issue to the UNSC for a second resolution of support in 2003 and the lack of public backlash when a second resolution was not acquired (on public reaction, see the following chapter). The importance of obtaining approval for domestic political reasons is apparent in the administration's prewar diplomatic calculations. The administration knew that getting a second resolution would likely have provided domestic political benefits. Woodward writes, "the administration viewed SC approval as a way to quiet the fears of U.S. business interests who were concerned about the impact of the war on the economy" (2004, 179; see also Marfleet and Miller 2005). Karl Rove, President George W. Bush's political advisor, admitted that although the "Republican base did not like the UN . . . it was necessary to try [to obtain its approval]" (Woodward 2004, 179). British Prime Minister Tony Blair similarly thought that obtaining Security Council support for the war would be critical for garnering public support, arguing to the Bush administration that a second resolution would be "an absolute political necessity" (297). Leaders clearly valued UNSC support because of its political benefits.

The fact that the value of authorization varies across institutions is also apparent in this diplomatic logic. Blair and others did not suggest that regional organization support was a "political necessity," but instead acted as if the authorization of the Security Council would result in the largest political benefit. Of course, NATO did not authorize the 2003 war and several NATO members voiced open opposition to the use of force, but concern seemed centered on making the case to the UN. Both NATO and the UNSC had veto-wielding members who voiced opposition to the use of force. Given public statements by these members, NATO may have also appeared conservative, illustrating the additional complexity of variation *within* institutions according to issue-specific preferences. Another possibility is that the opposition of NATO members was discounted because it did not involve a formal condemnation by the *institution* of NATO and was perceived as being driven more by non–policy-relevant concerns, such as French business ties to Iraq or antiwar European public opinion.

The value of institutional authorization, expressed by Rove, Blair, and others in 2003, is similar to George H. W. Bush's reasons for bringing the Iraq issue to the UNSC in 1990. His national security advisor, Brent Scowcroft, later wrote that, "The UN provided an added cloak of political cover . . . [it] was a political measure intended to seal international solidarity and strengthen domestic US support" (Bush and Scowcroft 1998, 416). Authorization also facilitated collective action, particularly for Arab allies, who wanted a "cover" from domestic political backlash (342). At the same time, obtaining authorization was made more vital by opposition from a Democratic Congress and wavering public approval numbers (Halberstam 2001, 15; Mueller 1994, 19). Bush writes, "The fall of 1990 was spent maintaining and strengthening our international coalition while building support at home for what we were doing . . . The domestic challenges were more complicated [than maintaining the coalition]. Foreign policy and budget politics mingled, becoming charged with partisanship as the mid-term elections approached" (Bush and Scowcroft 1998, 357). Internal memos detailing the White House communication plan during the fall of 1990 and early months of 1991 consistently emphasize mentioning UN Security Council support for the war.[2] For instance, talking points for the president's January 16, 1991, television address about the coming war mention the support of the UN Security Council as well as the Arab League.[3] The White House Bureau of Public Affairs also

---

2. Internal memos for Persian Gulf War from Bush Library Archives, Texas A&M University.
3. From Daniel Casse files, Bush Library.

planned a press conference in December 1990 in which ambassadors from twenty-six of the allied coalition stood with President Bush outside the White House and the president's comments underscored the coalition's support and agreement with the previously adopted UNSC resolutions.[4] Other internal memos focus on the need to emphasize the defensive nature of the action combined with UN support to assuage public fears.[5] Importantly, Security Council authorization was desired despite the existing support of key NATO allies, suggesting that the Security Council offered legitimacy benefits above and beyond that of a regional alliance comprised of traditional allies.

The political benefits of SC authorization were also likely at play in the Clinton administration's decision to push for an SC resolution authorizing intervention in Haiti in 1994. The need for legitimacy was perhaps even more pressing in this instance, as a conservative Congress made public support more difficult to obtain (Malone 1998; Schultz 2003) and the U.S. strategic and economic interests in Haiti may have been less clear. The costs to an administration of acting without public support likely increases during times of partisan opposition, and the public may have held very conservative preferences in this instance, particularly in the aftermath of the failures of the earlier Somalia intervention and "Black Hawk down" episode.[6]

The incentive to garner multilateral authorization for domestic political reasons is not limited to U.S. examples. As already mentioned, British Prime Minister Tony Blair pressured the Bush administration to make the case for invading Iraq to the UN in 2003. In a similar situation, French President François Mitterand wanted a formal Security Council resolution before French participation in the 1991 Persian Gulf War, fearing a domestic political backlash otherwise (Voeten 2005, 345).[7] Some governments make SC authorization a de facto prerequisite for participation in the use of force (Thompson 2006, 2). For instance, Australian intervention in East Timor in 1999 was made possible by SC authorization (Voeten 2005, 532; Coleman 2007). Germany, Japan, and Canada also routinely require SC authorization prior to contributing to military operations (Thompson 2006). German and

---

4. The initial memo from Deputy Assistant Secretary of Defense Daniel Kalinger to Special Assistant to the President for Communication Dave Demarest suggests showcasing the ambassadors. The press conference took place in the Rose Garden on December 17, 1990. Internal memos from the Iraq Working Group on the December 21 note that this conference was intended to bolster domestic and international support.

5. Memo from Richard Haas to John Sunu, November 28, 1990.

6. See Western (2002, 2005) on public reaction to Somalia.

7. Voeten cites then U.S. secretary of state James Baker's memoirs, which recount Mitterand's arguments the importance of SC authorization for French public opinion.

Japanese public opinion, in particular, are generally perceived as pacific due to the legacy of the destructiveness of World War II, and hence require some form of reassurance when their countries become involved in international disputes.

When comparing across types of states, it follows that because of greater domestic constraints democracies face stronger incentives to appeal to international organizations. This view differs from normative explanations for why democracies consult third parties during crises (cf. Dixon 1993; Raymond 1994). The normative argument suggests that democratic leaders seek third-party mediation because of norms of peaceful dispute settlement. The above model accords more closely with an institutional perspective of democratic behavior (e.g., Bueno de Mesquita et al. 1999). Specifically, democracies are more likely to consult multilateral organizations in order to loosen domestic constraints and pursue coercive policies.[8] However, democracies may also face greater incentives than other regime types to moderate their policy proposals in order to garner support from international institutions. This suggests that institutions can constrain aggression or encourage moderation through the channel of public opinion.

ALTERNATIVE NORMATIVE EXPLANATIONS

An alternative reason states appeal to international organizations for authorizing their policies is that it is the normatively appropriate thing to do. According to this explanation, states that have internal norms of peaceful conflict resolution will tend to appeal to third-party intermediaries—especially international institutions—for conflict resolution (Dixon 1993, 1994; Raymond 1994). This logic extends the normative strand of the democratic peace (Doyle 1986; Maoz and Russett 1993), which often argues that democracies are more pacific in general because they are founded on a principled belief in deliberation and peaceful resolution of disputes.

In contrast, structural theories of the democratic peace do not assume that democratic leaders are inherently less aggressive, only that democratic leaders wish to stay in office and that all populations pay some cost for international conflict (e.g., Bueno de Mesquita et al. 1999). In other words, states are distinguished not by their normative environments, but by whether their institutions hold leaders accountable to citizen preferences.[9] The institutional perspective has arguably received more empirical support, including

---

8. See Thompson (2006, 2009) and Chapman and Wolford (2010) for related points.
9. See Russett and Oneal 2001 for a review of the two approaches.

the well-established fact that democracies are no more peaceful in general than other regime types, and that democratic leaders appear to consider the public consequences of their actions more so than leaders in other regimes when choosing and fighting conflicts (Reiter and Stam 2002; Reiter and Meek 1999).

The informational argument is consistent with the institutional logic, but less so with the normative perspective. The informational logic makes no assumptions about the preferences of democratic leaders, except that they value undertaking foreign policy actions with public support. The informational logic of IOs and the institutional democratic peace both assume that citizens prefer lower-cost foreign policies to higher-cost ones. However, both the normative and informational perspective predict that democracies appeal to IOs more so than other states, but the normative perspective provides no prediction regarding the conditions under which democracies (or other states) are more or less likely to appeal to IOs, nor which IOs they might appeal to. The theory presented in chapter 2 suggests that leaders pick whether or not to consult an IO, and which IO to support, on the basis of whether and what kind of information its actions will convey to external audiences. These more nuanced and specific predictions are laid out below.

TESTABLE PREDICTIONS

There is substantial anecdotal evidence that domestic political factors have conditioned the decision of the United States and other countries to garner SC support in the post–cold war era. The logic provided in chapter 2 gives one answer for why SC support might help free up domestic constraints (Chapman and Reiter 2004), overcome domestic legislative opposition (Schultz 2003), or convey confidence to the public (Fang 2008). Namely, the Security Council, with multiple vetoing members with heterogeneous preferences, is likely to be perceived as relatively conservative in offering support for many foreign policy actions, including the use of force. Thus, if this institution is perceived to be even more conservative than the observer, then the an uncertain observer can conclude, upon seeing support for a policy, that the policy is likely to be one that the observer would also choose to support.

Given this logic, when is it likely that a leader would find it most necessary to convince uncertain domestic publics of the appropriateness of a proposed policy? Domestic institutions tend to create incentives for leaders to gain internal support. It has long been argued that leaders in countries with democratic institutions face incentives to enact popular policies. For instance, scholars have suggested that these incentives force leaders to choose to fight only winnable wars (Reiter and Stam 2002) and to provide adequate public goods to society (Bueno de Mesquita et al. 2003; Baum and Lake 2003). If leaders can be removed from office for undertaking unpopular foreign policy actions, it follows that these leaders should be more prone to try to assuage public confidence prior to undertaking those actions.[10] On the other hand, such leaders should avoid the opposition of institutions that are expected *ex ante* to support them. This logic suggests that democracies should be more likely to appeal to international organizations than nondemocracies.

The relationship between the proposing state's foreign policy preferences and the preferences of pivotal members of IOs is also critical to the predictions of the theory presented in chapter 2. In particular, the larger the distance between the two preferences, the more likely it is that support will signal the legitimacy of action while opposition will be discounted as uninformative. Therefore, the risk-return trade-off is the most attractive when the pivotal member holds preferences very far from the initiating state. However, chapter 2 predicted this relationship to exist only when leaders condition their behavior on public support, which is a function of the costliness of incurring public opposition. This cost is normally determined by how democratic a country's institutions are. This implies that the preference distance hypothesis is conditional on domestic institutions. These hypotheses constitute the most direct tests regarding the informational theory:

Hypothesis 1: Leaders are more likely to consult an international institution as the institution appears more distant in terms of foreign policy preferences.

Hypothesis 2: The effect of distance in foreign policy preferences is conditional on regime type. Democratic leaders are more likely to consult international institutions as ideological distance increases while nondemocratic leaders should be unresponsive to ideological distance.

When investigating these hypotheses it is important to account for other incentives to appeal to international security institutions. First, political conditions at the time of the crisis create added incentives for leaders to attempt to placate public opinion. Popular leaders may be given more leeway when conducting policy or dealing with their legislature (in the American

---

10. Huth and Allee (2006) claim that third-party dispute settlement provides political cover to democratic leaders. Tago (2005) suggests that U.S. presidents are more likely to see multilateral authorization during economic downturn or divided government.

context, see Fiorina 1981; Edwards 1980; Rivers and Rose 1985; Rhode and Simon 1985). One indicator of popularity that is available for a wide sample of countries in crises is the condition of the economy, as this indicator is often correlated with the incumbent popularity. Leaders should face a greater incentive to garner external support when the domestic economic faces an upturn in unemployment or inflation (see also Tago 2005).

A coordination or burden-sharing account would predict that countries in crises facing a relatively tough adversary attempt to garner the support of the SC in order to convince allies and their publics that they should join the conflict. One indicator of the severity of threat or likely costs of conflict is the relative capabilities of crisis adversaries. Alternatively, states that have a large advantage in terms of capabilities may deem multilateral assistance unnecessary. It is therefore important to control for relative capabilities, as coded by the International Crisis Behavior dataset. The next section lays out the data and design to test these predictions.

STATISTICAL ANALYSIS

This section presents two series of analyses testing the above predictions. The first set examines the determinants of appealing to the UN Security Council for all states during international crises from 1946 to 2003. The second set of analyses examines states' choice of whether to appeal to the Security Council or a relevant regional organization, introducing the possibility that states may forum shop and appeal to the IO that best accomplishes their goals. The second analysis necessarily reduces the number of cases examined, since not all states are members of regional consultative security organizations, whereas membership in the UN among crisis actors is nearly universal. Nonetheless, both analyses provide interesting evidence that the membership and preferences makeup of these bodies affects states' decisions to work through multilateral security institutions.

The International Crisis Behavior (ICB) project (Brecher and Wilkenfeld 2006) identifies all foreign policy crises faced by sovereign states and documents characteristics of the crisis and the political actors involved. From 1946 to 2003, the ICB project recorded 439 distinct international crises, defined as an event in which decision makers "perceive[d] a threat to basic values, time pressure for response and a heightened probability of military hostilities" (Brecher and Wilkenfeld 2006, 18). The ICB project further designates crisis actors, those who were direct participants in each crisis. Between 1946 and 2003, there were 727 "actor-level observations," one case for each country involved in the 439 distinct crises. Each of the "actor-level observations" in this study can be thought of as an opportunity for a state to consult an international organization. The following analysis uses this data to look at the conditions under which countries choose to consult the UN or other organizations when confronted with these opportunities.

The first set of results examines whether a country appealed in any way to the UN Security Council. Appeals are judged by examining descriptions of the crises and related historical sources. Among all the opportunities in this dataset, there are ninety-four instances of a country appealing to the UN Security Council. These "appeals" simply mean that the state formally requested the IO to discuss the crisis in question or submitted a resolution for consideration.

The second set of results looks at whether a country appealed to either a regional security organization or the UN Security Council when confronted with a crisis. There are thirty-seven instances of a country taking an issue to a regional organization in this set of cases. Like above, appeals consist of a country either formally requesting an IO to discuss a crisis or submitting a resolution for consideration.

The test of hypotheses 1 and 2, the core hypotheses of the informational account, requires some indicator of the relative foreign policy preferences of IOs and states conducting foreign policy. One frequently used measure of foreign policy preference similarity is the S score, developed by Signorino and Ritter (1999). S is a measure ranging from −1 to 1, based on how frequently two countries vote together in the UN General Assembly. It is a measure of voting distance in a multidimensional space, where scores closer to 1 indicate more affinity in voting patterns while scores closer to −1 indicate less affinity. The S score is a reasonable summary measure of how closely two countries' foreign policy preferences are.

This measure is not unproblematic as a general measure of relative preferences. Voting in the General Assembly can be strategic, but is often treated as relatively sincere, since it is dominated by smaller states and its decisions are nonbinding (see Voeten 2000, 2005).[11] It is thus common to treat these votes as "sincere," or revealing of the preferences of member states.[12] To measure a state's relative preference relationship with the UN Security

11. Gartzke (1998) uses this measure as a proxy of "similarity of interests." See also Stone 2004 and Oatley and Yackee 2004 for uses of this measure.
12. I also assume that states are not making side payments for votes in the General Assembly. Although this may occur, it is much more likely in the SC where decisions carry more weight. In addition, it is not clear that strategic voting would bias these scores in any systematic way; rather, the possibility of strategic voting would simply introduce substantial measurement error, working against finding strong relationships in the expected direction.

Council, we can use each state's S score with the most distant permanent member. This member represents the "pivotal member" from each state's point of view, as this is the member least likely to support that state's initiatives. In institutions that operate with a majority rule, the pivotal member is the median of all voting members in a given year. Thus, each country has a *unique* S score relative to each institution in a given year.

A separate critique of this measure of preferences is that it may not capture any particular underlying, latent preference dimension. This is a relevant concern for any measure that attempts to place political actors along some preference dimension. In this context, however, many authors have found that voting patterns in the General Assembly are typically characterized by one or two dimensions (see Russet and Kim 1996; Voeten 2000), and Voeten shows that since the cold war voting in the General Assembly can be represented along one dimension, with the United States at one pole. This makes the S score a reasonable indicator of foreign policy distance, corresponding to the theoretical model from chapter 2.

In order to see whether preference relationship matters only for more democratic countries, we can combine the S score with a measure of democracy. One commonly used indicator of a country's level of democracy is the Polity IV regime-type measure. The measure arranges countries from autocratic to democratic, assigning numerical values to characterize the country's political institutions. The resulting scale ranges from −10 (most autocratic) to 10 (most democratic). If the need to obtain political cover by consulting a more distant IO is mostly a characteristic of more democratic countries, we should see the effect of the S score increase as the Polity scale increases. These two measures are combined by multiplying them together in an interaction term, which can be used to test a conditional relationship.

The remaining control variables come from the ICB project data, with the exception of the regime score. Power disparity is a continuous variable measuring the difference in power capabilities between the crisis actor and the adversary, ranging from −179 (least favorable for the crisis actor) to 179 (most favorable). Power disparity is meant to account for the possibility that states appeal to IOs for assistance and to garner allies in order to lessen the power disparity between themselves and an adversary. I also include binary measures from the ICB project data indicating whether the state experienced a marked increase in unemployment or inflation prior to the onset of the crisis. Although crude, these measures serve as indicators of the likely political position of the regime in power prior to the crisis, a proxy for the extent to which the regime deems it necessary to acquire public support for foreign policy. These variables are also combined with the Polity score, as the effect of these domestic factors on the need for public support, and thus multilateral authorization, should be greater for democracies. Finally, I include a measure of the seriousness of the threat to the crisis actor, called "gravity." This measure ranges from economic threat (0) to threat to existence (7). The expectation is that states are more likely to seek out multilateral support for more serious threats, as responses to such threats are more likely to be costly and require public support.

APPEALING TO THE SECURITY COUNCIL

The results look at when countries appealed to the Security Council during the crises identified from 1946 to 2003. Table 3.1 shows the coefficient, or estimated relationship, between each variable and the probability of making an appeal. These coefficients are generated by a probit estimation, which is commonly employed when the outcome of interest can only take on two values (appeal or no appeal).[13]

The most important results to note are the coefficients on the interaction term between regime type and foreign policy similarity with the UN Security Council, as well as the estimates on each of the individual variables. Model 1 displays the S score interacted with the Polity scale. The coefficient for the S score alone represents the effect of similarity when the Polity regime-type score equals 0. The theory predicts little effect of similarity for these types of regimes, and this is borne out by the data, in that this coefficient indicates little effect of preference similarity/distance on appeals to the Security Council. The coefficient for the polity score represents the effect of the polity score when similarity is equal to 0 (and when unemployment and inflation are also equal to 0). The theory predicts that democracies should have greater incentives to obtain institutional authorization regardless of similarity, and this is also borne out by the data, as indicated by the positive and significant coefficient for regime type.

The coefficient on the interaction term suggests an interesting dynamic, however. First, when the S score and the Polity score are both negative, in other words when the informational benefit of authorization is high but the state in question is more autocratic and less in need of public support, there should be little effect. When both are positive—in other words, when the

13. The models are estimated using robust standard errors clustered by crisis to account for nonindependence in the behavior of multiple actors involved in the same crisis.

state is more democratic and desires public support but the potential informational benefit of the signal is low—there should also be little effect. When the S score is negative and the regime-type score positive, however, a state should be more likely to appeal to the Security Council, as the state will be more desirous of public support and face a positive informational risk-return trade-off with respect to obtaining Security Council authorization. This is reflected in the data. When one term is negative and the other positive and is multiplied by a negative coefficient, there is a positive effect on the probability of appealing to the Security Council. Otherwise, there is a negative effect. In other words, more democratic states are more likely to consult the Security Council as it becomes more distant, which supports the informational argument.

Figure 3.1 displays estimated marginal effect of democracy on the probability of consulting the Security Council at various levels of similarity to the council. When similarity is very high, meaning that the risk-return trade-off of consultation is not very appealing, higher levels of democracy are not strongly associated with higher probabilities of consultations. In other words, more democratic countries are not any more likely to consult the

TABLE 3.1   Analysis of UN Security Council consultations, 1946–2003

VARIABLE	MODEL 1
S	−.236 (.226)
Polity democracy score	−.007 (.023)
S*Polity	−.063* (.030)
Power disparity	−.005 (.002)*
Unemployment	.041 (.032)
Unemployment*Polity democracy score	.008 (.005)
Inflation	.058 (.047)
Inflation*Polity democracy score	.004 (.007)
Gravity	−.014 (.065)
Constant	−1.328 (.268)
N	418
Log likelihood	−169.514
χ^2	25.61**

Note: Robust standard errors clustered by crisis: 185 clusters.
*.10; 1-tailed p values.
**.05; 1-tailed p values.

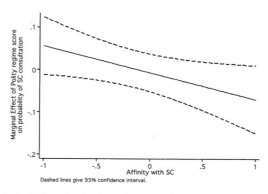

FIGURE 3.1   Marginal effect of regime by preference similarity

Security Council when there is not a large expected benefit. However, as similarity decreases, more democratic countries become much more likely to consult the Security Council. This is supportive of the idea that when a country is distant in terms of foreign policy preferences from the council it faces a more favorable risk-reward trade-off, in that the potential backlash associated with opposition is less likely to be costly while the potential political benefits of support are likely to be large.

Table 3.2 shows the estimated probability of consulting the Security Council for different types of countries in a crisis based on these estimations.[14] The categories of "pure democracy" and "pure autocracy" and the corresponding levels of similarity to the Security Council represent ideal types and not any specific country. However, based on the statistical estimations we can say something about the relative likelihood that these hypothetical countries would choose to consult the Security Council during a crisis. All else being equal, there is about a 15 percent chance that a strong democracy will consult the Security Council during a crisis if its similarity to the pivotal member is about neutral, or if they vote with that member just about as frequently as the vote against it. If we consider the extreme case, however, when the democracy always votes against the pivotal member (S score of −1), there is about a 35 percent chance of consulting the SC. The likelihood of consultation increases dramatically with preference distance, supporting the idea that the risk-return trade-off of consultation actually improves with this distance.

14. These probabilities are obtained by holding all other variables at their means.

TABLE 3.2   Predicted probability of Security Council consultation

POLITY SCORE/SC SIMILARITY SCORE	NEUTRAL SIMILARITY TO SC (S SCORE = 0)	LOW SIMILARITY WITH SC (S SCORE = −1)
"Pure democracy" (Polity score of 10)	14.7%	35.5%
"Pure autocracy" (Polity score of −10)	18.2%	9.1%

For a country on the opposite extreme of the institutional spectrum, a strongly autocratic state, we see no such pattern. In fact, the opposite pattern appears to be the case, although because of rather large confidence intervals on the estimates for the autocratic state we cannot have much confidence about this difference.[15] An autocratic state with a more or less neutral relationship with the pivotal member of the Security Council has about an 18 percent chance of making a consultation, while a similar state with a more distant preferential relationship with the Security Council has about half as high a chance of consultation. Autocratic regimes have less of a need to acquire political cover for their policies, and this is borne out in the data.

Turning to other control variables, the results are mixed. The effect of unemployment when regime type is equal to zero is to increase the likelihood of appealing to the Security Council, providing some limited support for the notion that even mixed regimes respond to domestic incentives to improve the popularity of foreign policies. However, neither a recent increase in inflation nor the interactions between unemployment and regime type yield significant results. Interestingly, the coefficient on the interaction term between inflation and regime type suggests that inflation results in a lower probability of appealing to the Security Council, which is counterintuitive if one believes that inflation is political unpopular. Inflation should make regimes more likely to seek external legitimization during crises if those regimes desire public support for foreign policies. Nonetheless, political scientists have only crude measures of the forces that imperil regimes, particularly mixed and autocratic regimes, despite a large and increasingly sophisticated body of literature on the nature of autocratic rule.[16] One can-

15. Confidence intervals on the predictions of 18.2% and 9.1% for autocratic states are [7.1%, 36%] and [1%, 31%], respectively. The key point is that there are not significant differences in the probability of consultation for nondemocracies.
16. See Brownlee 2007, Gandhi 2008.

not rule out that regimes respond to domestic political unrest by obtaining external legitimization for foreign policies, although the data analyzed here provide no support for this notion.

Finally, the data support the expectation that states are less likely to consult the Security Council when the power disparity is large and in their favor. The opposite holds true as well; weak states consult the Security Council, perhaps for coalition building incentives. This is confirmation of the burden-sharing argument—that states seek institutional multilateralism when the potential costs of conflict are high. This topic is taken up in more detail in chapter 5.

FORUM SHOPPING—THE SECURITY COUNCIL AND REGIONAL ORGANIZATIONS

The Security Council, although often the first IO to come to mind when states face severe crises, is not the only outlet states have available for obtaining external legitimization. Many states belong to regional organizations that have similar consultative functions, such as the OAS, the Organization of African Unity (OAU, now the African Union), or even NATO. If states choose to appeal to the Security Council when its support is politically most helpful and its opposition is politically least costly, might they also choose between the Security Council and possible regional forums using a similar reasoning?

The anecdotal evidence of this dynamic is quite limited and what exists initially appears to show an opposite association. For instance, in 1999 the United States avoided operating through the Security Council when conducting airstrikes in Kosovo in order to avoid a Russian veto, despite a public preference for working through the Security Council. This seems to run counter to the logic suggested above, in that the United States worked through NATO out of convenience and burden-sharing rather than out of need for collective legitimization. However, in other contexts, such as the first Gulf War, the United States invested substantial time in acquiring Security Council authorization although the operation would likely have enjoyed clear support from NATO allies. In other scenarios, such as U.S. intervention in Grenada, the United States sought regional organization support in order to placate opinion in the region. And one reason the Security Council is often the venue of choice may be because it is seen as having a higher "legislative hurdle," meaning that its support is more valued than regional organizations, which may be seen as more uniformly biased toward particularly states. Nonetheless, there may be situations in which the sanction of a particular regional organization is seen as critical, such as the elder Bush administration's courtship of the Arab League prior to the first Gulf War.

There is quite a bit of interest in forum shopping in other political contexts. Political actors often appear to strategically choose which institutions to act through, even creating new rules that serve their political goals (Jupille 2004; Busch 2007). Following this logic, states may be expected to choose security venues in order to maximize their goals at a given point in time. In some contexts, these goals may be first and foremost acquiring allies, such as the United States in the Kosovo campaign. In other contexts, the foremost goal may be making a political point and gaining political support, in which case states may appeal to the available institution that is further from their own interests.

The following statistical analysis examines the forum shopping incentives of states in foreign policy crises. Specifically, the analysis looks at which factors cause countries to appeal to the UN Security Council *or* a relevant regional organization. If the two are partial substitutes, then states face a trade-off between appealing to the organization that will provide the largest political benefit versus an organization from which they may be more likely to acquire support. Here again the key variable of interest is the similarity to the pivotal member in each organization, although now the additional variable of similarity to the appropriate regional organization is included. To preserve an appropriate comparison, the data consist of only states that belong both to the UN and to a regional consultative security organization, including the OAS, OAU, NATO, the Southeast Asia Treaty Organization (SEATO), and the League of Arab States (LAS, or, Arab League).

Since states have several options for securing approval, the data distinguish between the state choosing not to appeal to an IO, appealing to a regional organization, or appealing to the Security Council.[17] I include the same control variables as the previous analysis.

Table 3.3 displays the results of the forum shopping analysis. The results provide some limited support for the forum shopping argument, in that states seem to appeal to the multilateral organization that will provide the strongest signal of foreign policy legitimacy to their audience. First, con-

17. There are nine instances in the entire dataset of a state appealing to both the Security Council and a regional organization. After accounting for missing data on the similarity score (for years in dyadic General Assembly voting is unavailable), there are three cases of a state appealing to both the Security Council and a regional organization. Estimating a multinomial choice model on the alternative four category-dependent variables (no appeal, regional organization appeal, SC appeal, or both regional organization and SC appeal) does not yield substantively different results.

TABLE 3.3   Multinomial logit results

INDEPENDENT VARIABLES	SECURITY COUNCIL CONSULTATION	REGIONAL ORGANIZATION CONSULTATION
Security Council Affinity	−1.241 (.801)	−1.716* (.798)
Regime Type	.017 (.063)	−.034 (.056)
Regime Type*Security Council Affinity	−.239* (.107)	−.123 (.114)
Regional Organization Affinity	.514 (.660)	.102 (.667)
Regime Type*Regional Organization Affinity	.116 (.077)	.102 (.097)
Power Disparity	−.015 (.010)	.006 (.003)
Unemployment	−.0002 (.0729)	−.100 (.091)
Inflation	.064 (.073)	.120 (.092)
Constant	−2.045 (.547)	−2.961 (.574)
χ^2	25.27	
N	297.	
Log pseudolikelihood	−192.702	

Note: Coefficients are reported with robust standard errors in parentheses. Standard errors are clustered by crisis to account for nonindependence.
*Significant at the .05 level.

sider the effect of the interaction term between the similarity of the state to the Security Council and the state's regime type. Recall from the earlier analysis that this coefficient was negative—meaning that when a country's regime score becomes more positive (more democratic) and the similarity between the country and the SC becomes more negative (less similar), the state is more likely to appeal to the Security Council. This coefficient remains negative in the multinomial model for the category of appealing to the Security Council, but narrowly misses statistical significance with a p value of .104 with a 1-tailed hypothesis test. However, the coefficient for this interaction displays the opposite sign with regard to appealing to regional organizations. In other words, when more democratic states have more in common with the Security Council they are more likely to turn to regional organizations during crises. The two appear to be operating as "informational substitutes," in the sense that states trade-off prestige for the credibility of a signal of support. When Security Council authorization is not as beneficial for democratic states, they may turn to regional organizations that provide a better, or more credible, signal of the merits of foreign policy.

Next, consider the effect of similarity to regional organizations. The findings with regard to how regional organization similarity affects appeals to regional organizations are mixed, showing only that mixed regimes (regime = 0) are more likely to appeal to regional organizations as their similarity with the organization increases. This is indicated by the coefficient on regional organization similarity, which should be interpreted as the effect of similarity when regime is equal to zero. However, regional organization similarity tends to have a positive effect both for mixed regimes and for more democratic regimes when it comes to appealing to the Security Council, as indicated by the coefficients for regional organization similarity and the interaction with regime type for the Security Council outcome. In other words, states tend to appeal to the Security Council when they share more in common with their respective regional organization and as they become more democratic. This supports the notion that states face incentives to appeal to organizations that are not anticipated to support them *ex ante*. When the available regional organization is expected to support them because of a close foreign policy affinity, states tend to turn to the Security Council.

Table 3.4 shows the predicted probability that hypothetical pure democracies and pure autocracies would appeal to regional organizations or the Security Council at various levels of similarity with the Security Council. The results are very similar to those in table 3.2, which showed the probability of consultation only to the Security Council. Again, there is little evidence that autocracies are more likely to appeal to a more distant Security Council. In fact, the opposite appears true as it did in table 3.2: autocracies are more likely to consult a "friendlier" Security Council, although this probability is not statistically significant from that under a neutral similarity score. However, the hypothetical pure democracy appears much more likely to consult the Security Council when it is less similar. Democracies and nondemocracies appear to operate with different logics, as the theory in chapter 2 suggested. Democracies seek out the Security Council when

TABLE 3.4   Predicted probabilities of forum shopping

	NEUTRAL SIMILARITY WITH SC (s = 0)		LOW SIMILARITY WITH SC (s = −1)		HIGH SIMILARITY WITH SC (s=1)	
	REGIONAL	SC	REGIONAL	SC	REGIONAL	SC
"Pure democracy" (Polity IV score = 10)	7.5%	22.0%	23.0%	61.0%	2.4%	2.6%
"Pure autocracy" (polity IV score = −10)	10.7%	10.0%	20.0%	5.1%	7.0%	24.0%

TABLE 3.5   Bivariate probit forum shopping

	SECURITY COUNCIL CONSULTATION	REGIONAL ORGANIZATION CONSULTATION
Security Council affinity	−.415 (.355)	−.724* (.359)
Regime type	.017 (.030)	−.013 (.026)
Regime type*Security Council affinity	−.115 (.040)	−.035 (.053)
Regional organization affinity	.152 (.343)	.910* (.317)
Regime type*regional organization affinity	.051 (.041)	.034 (.056)
Power disparity	−.008 (.005)	.003 (.001)
Unemployment	.003 (.036)	−.051 (.045)
Inflation	.025 (.038)	.055 (.047)
Constant	−1.171 (.284)	−1.722 (.261)
ρ	.085 (.162)	
χ^2	28.43	
N	297	
Log pseudolikelihood	−204.28096	

Note: Robust standard errors clustered by crisis.
*Significant at the .05 level.

its political benefits are highest, while autocracies appear unconcerned with the informational benefits of approval.

The results regarding the other control variables are again quite mixed; the data say little about the relationship between domestic economic conditions and the incentives for external legitimization.

One disadvantage to the multinomial logit framework is the assumption of independent and irrelevant alternatives. The logit framework makes the rather strong assumption that the odds of choosing one alternative are independent of the presence of the other alternatives (Long 1997, 182), which is dubious in the presence of strategic considerations. Table 3.5 thus provides results from an alternative, the seemingly unrelated bivariate probit estimator, which allows correlation in the error structure of the two equations. There are no clear substantive differences between the two analyses.[18] The negative sign on the coefficient for Security Council similarity with respect

18. Note that ρ is not statistically significant in the bivariate probit estimation, suggesting that the errors of the two equations are not correlated.

to consulting a regional organization suggests that as states come closer to the Security Council in terms of preference similarity they are more likely to consult their respective regional organization. This is further support for the informational forum shopping argument and contradicts the view that states simply seek out the organization that is most likely to offer its support. On the other hand, regional organization affinity displays a positive and significant coefficient in the regional organization consultation equation, suggesting that states may consult regional organizations when they are more ideologically similar. The example of the United States seeking OECS authorization for the Grenada invasion demonstrates this logic. In the face of expected opposition from the Security Council and the OAS, the United States turned to an IO that was highly likely to approve its actions. Although this provided some political cover, the end result was little international legitimacy, largely because the ploy of obtaining cover from a "friendly" group of states was transparent to domestic and foreign audiences.

DISCUSSION AND CONCLUSION

Previous research on why states work through security organizations has focused on either general institutionalist explanations (coordination, commitment) or normative moral or legal explanations (legitimization, peaceful dispute resolution). The informational logic put forth in chapter 2 suggests an alternative—that states use international security organizations in order to communicate policy-relevant information to their publics. The degree to which this information influences audiences is determined by the preferences of member states in international organizations. In particular, when those preferences are arrayed such that it is relatively difficult to obtain a supportive decision, such a decision is particularly effective at providing "political cover," perhaps facilitating coordination.

This chapter presented two tests of the informational incentives to appeal to the Security Council and regional organizations. Specifically I examined whether the distance in policy preferences between a proposing state and the pivotal member of an international organization (from that state's point of view), as measured by UN General Assembly voting records, affects the decision to appeal to that organization for supportive decisions during crises.

The initial test focused on when all states involved in international crises from 1946 to 2003 appealed to the UN Security Council. The findings suggest that the informational incentive is stronger as states become more democratic. These states face the largest public opinion constraints and therefore have the greatest need to obtain external legitimization for foreign policies.

When examining whether states might choose between different forums for obtaining this legitimization, the results provide some support that regional organizations and the UN Security Council may act as informational substitutes for states. States tend to appeal to the organization that is more dissimilar in terms of foreign policy positions because these organizations are best equipped to confer legitimacy on foreign policies. Perhaps the most interesting result is that not only does the relationship of a state to a particular IO determine whether it appeals to that IO, but so too does the relationship of a state to *other IOs*. States tend to approach the Security Council when a regional organization is likely to provide only a "noisy" signal because of its foreign policy affinity to the state. Likewise, when the pivotal member of the Security Council holds preferences more similar to the state, the state is more likely to approach a regional organization. These results shed new light on the determinants of global or regional multilateralism.

What do these results say more generally for the role of security organizations? Can these organizations constrain powerful states? On the one hand, it is clear that powerful states, including the United States, view the authorization of the UN Security Council as valuable, particularly because the council does not always agree with them. This likely forces states to moderate proposals for the use of force, consider the implications of unilateral action before using force, and make efforts to persuade the international community that proposed uses of force will not be overly expansive. On the other hand, approval of an IO may alleviate or eliminate critical disincentives to use force, such as concern of international retaliation or a domestic backlash. Paradoxically, the presence of these institutions may force moderation while at the same time facilitating coercion via authorization.[19]

Which of these outcomes obtains depends critically on the makeup of the institution. Since the value of obtaining authorization depends on the distance in preferences between aggressor states and the pivotal member of the organization, who that member is for each state plays a large role in determining how much states value obtaining authorization. When that authorization is valuable, as it has appeared to be for the United States with regard to the Security Council, the institution will be relatively effective at forcing moderation and compromise. However, as chapter 2 suggested, when the pivotal member of an institution is closely aligned with an aggressor state, although support is less valuable, opposition can be costly. Moreover, states will tend to avoid policies that will receive opposition from closely aligned

19. On this point see Thompson 2009 and Chapman and Wolford 2010.

institutions altogether. Thus, the trade-offs in institutional design focus on the value of authorization, versus the potential costs of opposition.

The next chapter considers the effect of organizational activity on public opinion in the United States, building on the informational logic developed in chapter 2 and the evidence provided here.

APPENDIX: A NOTE ON SAMPLE SELECTION

Selection bias is an ever-present consideration in the study of crisis behavior and thus merits discussion.[20] Scholars have amply demonstrated that failure to take into account the factors that lead to observations' inclusion in a sample can cause biased parameter estimates if those factors are correlated with core independent variables (Heckman 1979; Signorino 2002). The insight that strategic behavior, in particular, may cause this type of specification error has prompted significant attention in recent years (cf. Signorino 1999; Signorino and Yilmaz 2003; Signorino and Tarar 2006; Smith 1999; Carrubba, Yuen, and Zorn 2008). Failing to account for the nonrandom sample selection may lead to faulty inferences about actors' behavior in crises.

I have thus far treated the ICB data as a random sample of opportunities to consult the UN Security Council. However, this assumption would be faulty if the sample is nonrandom with respect to independent variables of interest. In other words, one must ask whether the factors that cause crisis onset might systematically bias inferences regarding the effect of similarity on the decision to appeal to the Security Council. In particular, if actors only initiate crises when they are already distant from the Security Council in terms of foreign policy preferences (or highly similar) one might incorrectly infer that foreign policy distance leads to consultation.

There are several ways to address this concern. First, it is important to note that crises have diverse causes, and many crises occur without initiation by the party that ultimately appeals to a multilateral organization. Thus, if strategic anticipation of the political benefits of multilateral support affect crisis onset, it would likely only occur in a small subset of cases. Empirically, since the ICB data define a crisis as a "perceived threat"—that is, perceived by the crisis actor—most examples of IO consultations involve the threatened crisis actor consulting the IO. The key point is that the consulter, or threatened actor, is not the crisis initiator.

However, if crises are defined for some actors when their adversaries respond to an initial provocation, it remains possible that decision to initiate is linked to later decisions to consult. This would likely affect only a subset of cases, such as those in which public opinion dependent leaders would otherwise avoid crisis situations unless they anticipate a political boost from multilateral support. To the extent that these situations are likely to be rare, the possibility of selection is unlikely to affect the results in chapter 3.

20. For examples of treatments see Danilovic 2001, Fearon 2002, Meernick 2000, Smith 1998, Kinsella and Russett 2002, and Reed 2000.

RESOLUTION* PASSED	DECISION TYPE**	RESOLUTION NUMBER(S)
1	1	2
1	1	15
1	1	38, 39, 47, 51
0	0	None
0	0	None
0	0	None
1	2	82, (see also 83–85 authorizing force)
1	1	92
0	0	None
0	0	None
0	0	None
1	2	106
0	0	None
0	0	None
0	0	None
0	0	None
1	1	128
1	2	143
0	0	None
1	1	164
0	0	None
1	1	No record in UN docs
0	0	None
1	1	186, 193
0	0	None
0	0	None
0	0	None
1	1	203
1	2	216
0	0	None
1	1	244
0	0	None
0	0	None

RESOLUTION* PASSED	DECISION TYPE**	RESOLUTION NUMBER(S)
1	2	300
1	2	326–329
1	1	339, 340
1	1	353–355, 357–361
1	1	377, 379–380
0	0	None
1	1	395
1	2	403, 406
1	2	411
0	0	None
0	0	None
1	2	425, 426
1	2	428
0	0	None
1	2	447
0	0	None
1	1 (could possibly be a "weak" 2 or 3)	457
1	2	475
0	0	None
0	0	None
0	0	None
0	0	None
1	2	527
0	0	None
1	2	545
0	0	None
0	0	None
0	0	None
1	1	582
0	0	None
0	0	None
0	0	None

(continued)

TABLE 3A.1   *(continued)*

RESOLUTION* PASSED	DECISION TYPE**	RESOLUTION NUMBER(S)
1	2	602
1	1	644
1	2	678 (see also 677, 661–662, 664–667, 674, 677–678)
0	0	None
1	1	854, 858
0	0	None
1	2	852
0	0	None
1	2	940
1	2	949
1	2	1052 (April 18)
0	0	None
1	2	1154
1	2	1205
1	2	1368, 1378 (after the war)
0	0	None
0	0	None

Note: All Security Council appeals, decision, and resolution numbers.
*Resolutions are coded as follows: 0 = not passed, 1 = passed.
**Decision types are coded as follows: 0 = no decision, 1 = neutral, 2 = in favor of appealing party, 3 = in favor of other state.

Notably, there is little evidence of selection bias in other tests of whether domestic political factors affect U.S. decisions to obtain multilateral authorization for foreign policy actions (Tago 2005). Instead, the initial occurrence of military disputes and international crises appear to be independent of the later political decisions to consult multilateral organizations.

4

UN AUTHORIZATION AND U.S. PUBLIC OPINION

Why are the decisions of international organizations sometimes treated as legitimate by domestic observers? Chapter 2 provided one answer: because of pervasive uncertainty surrounding international events, actors look for additional sources of information when making decisions. The domestic public, for instance, may seek to acquire information about either foreign policies or the leaders who propose them when deciding whether they should support their elected leaders (Chapman and Reiter 2004; Fang 2008; Grieco 2003). Audiences in other states may want reassurance that states will not act overly aggressively when conducting foreign policy (Voeten 2005) or may acquire information about the resolve of states that receive multilateral support (Thompson 2006; Chapman and Wolford, 2010). Importantly, these mechanisms can help constrain the behavior of leaders who propose foreign policies to change the international status quo, as they face incentives to moderate policies in order to garner IO support.[1] Leaders face a trade-off between making compromises in order to obtain the benefits of institutional authorization and eschewing multilateral fetters in favor of policy autonomy.

---

1. See Dai 2005 for a theory of domestic political incentives for compliance with international regimes. Schultz (2003) argues that U.S. presidents have used IOs to override domestic opposition.

In chapter 2 I demonstrated that behavior consistent with legitimacy, or the belief that an institution's decisions should be followed (Hurd 1999), is conditional on the preferences and strategic behavior of member states within an institution. When consultative security bodies hold aggregate preferences that are perceived to be generally opposed to the foreign policy goals of a proposing state, support or authorization from those bodies is a powerful signal to an uninformed audience that a proposed policy is worth supporting. While the effect of IO support on public support for foreign policies is expected to *increase* as ideological similarity between members of the institution and the proposing state *decreases*, the effect of IO opposition (or failure to garner support) is expected to *increase* as that similarity *increases*. Bodies whose aggregate interests tend to be inimical to a proposing state can provide an uninformed audience with a strong signal of policy suitability. Bodies that are clearly friendly to a state's interests can provide an uninformed audience with a strong signal of the dangers of a proposed foreign policy by expressing their (unexpected) disapproval.

These theoretical claims account for a great deal of previously unexplained variation in observed reactions to institutional decisions. Public and foreign reactions to decisions clearly vary across institutions (e.g., Security Council vs. OAS); within institutions over time (e.g., Security Council pre- and post–cold war); and across observers (e.g., American and European reactions to the Security Council decisions regarding Iraq in 2002–2003). Yet most explanations for why this variation exists are post hoc, inferring, for instance, that UN authorization is considered more legitimate than that of other IOs simply because we see individuals act like it is. Unfortunately, this is not a falsifiable explanation of organizational influence.

In addition to providing predictions about public response to IO decisions, the informational logic leads to the counterintuitive conclusion that if governments care about domestic support for foreign policies, they face incentives to appeal to *less friendly* institutions. In other words, instead of seeking political "cover" for foreign policy actions by appealing to organizations that are clearly expected to offer support, governments face incentives to appeal to institutions that are predisposed to oppose them. Winning support from such institutions provides a boon for public support, while opposition from such bodies does not automatically decrease public support. The data analysis in chapter 3 provided support for this idea.

This chapter investigates the political incentives behind such behavior. Specifically, this chapter presents evidence about the U.S. public's reaction to IO activity during U.S. military disputes and discusses some explanations for patterns surrounding prominent foreign policy events of the last twenty years. I build on earlier work on the "rally 'round the flag" effect (Chapman and Reiter 2004) but add the conditional expectation that rallies are larger when accompanied by more informative signals from multilateral bodies. This provides additional support for the informational logic, which suggests that IO influence is conditional on observers' beliefs about member state motives.

INFORMATION TRANSMISSION AND PUBLIC OPINION

To review the theory presented in chapter 2, recall that behavior consistent with a legitimacy view, such as the frequent decision by governments to seek multilateral authorization or a domestic audience reacting to authorization with increased support for their leader, may be due to the information conveyed by institutional activity to key audiences, such as the domestic or foreign public. For instance, Voeten (2005) suggests that the UNSC possesses few of the characteristics—policy neutrality, inclusiveness, procedural fairness—that tend to lead to perceptions of legitimacy. Instead, Voeten suggests that authorization signals that powerful states will not oppose a foreign policy, which lowers expectations of costs for domestic audiences and signals that policies will not be overly expansive to foreign audiences. Thompson (2006) offers a related theory, claiming that powerful states seek authorization for coercive purposes because it signals benign intent to foreign audiences, lowering international opposition.

In a formal model with similar themes to the one presented in chapter 2, Fang (2008) examines how the decision to seek multilateral authorization can signal a leader's competence to domestic audiences. Rational leaders should anticipate whether they will receive IO support or opposition, implying that incompetent leaders will often avoid consulting an IO and revealing their "type." In turn, the public should be more likely to support leaders who consult an international organization like the UNSC, because it signals that they are competent, in the sense they are likely to implement good policies.

Chapter 2 argued that IO authorization can signal whether proposed policies are "good," in the sense that they conform closely to the public's preferences, but adds the caveat that the effect of authorization on domestic support for policies should be conditional on an audience's perceptions of the interests of an organization's member states, who drive organizational decisions. In other words, audiences that are relatively uninformed about international affairs may seek information about foreign policy when forming their opinions, but must "consider the source," just as they would when listening to politicians or media pundits arguing for domestic policies. A citizen who cares only about good policy may discount arguments about the value of tax cuts from a Republican senator with a record of arguing for "small government," while the same citizens may take similar arguments from a Democratic senator with a record of supporting public spending as an important signal about the need for tax cuts.[2] The analysis suggested an analogous process should operate when citizens observe signals from international organizations. Organizations comprised of member states that are predisposed to veto a given resolution communicate little about policy merit when they oppose policies, as they are expected to do so. However, support from such member states can convince audiences that a policy is worth supporting. The opposite is true for organizations that are comprised of "friends" or traditional allies of a proposing state; opposition is an unexpected and strong signal that a given policy may be costly or overly aggressive, while support conveys little information about policy appropriateness because it is expected.

Of course, in general models of information transmission between a principal (receiver) and an agent (sender), "truth-telling" or "information revealing" equilibria occur when the principal and agent have identical preferences. In such a situation what is good for the agent is also good for the principal, and since the agent has no interest in provoking outcomes that are bad, the agent's signals can typically be trusted. This situation may sometimes be true when states receive signals from very close allies. For instance, Kydd (2003) points out that Serbian leaders took Russian signals about U.S. resolve very seriously during the 1999 Kosovo operation, since Russian and Serb preferences were closely correlated. However, in many cases this is not possible, such as in Kydd's alternative example of the Argentine military junta, which discounted American signals about British resolve during the 1982 Falkland Islands crisis. Since the United States was a close ally to the UK, it could be expected to try to convince the Argentines to back down, regardless of whether Britain actually intended to follow through with a military conflict.

An identical logic can be applied to signals from IOs, whose decisions are driven by member states that often have a stake in the outcomes of the issues under consideration. Opposition is likely to be "noisy" or reveal very little information, as long as it comes from an IO whose members' interests are distant from a state proposing foreign policy action. On the other hand, support from such an institution is likely to be more convincing when relevant

2. Gilligan and Krehbiel (1988, 1990) develop similar ideas about committee structures in Congress.

members' interests are distant from a proposing state, because the members have no interest in supporting policies that will create bad outcomes from their point of view. From the point of view of ordinary citizens, support from an organization comprised solely of allies has the opposite problem—it is expected to occur under a variety of circumstances, some of which may be prohibitively costly from the point of view of citizens.

We can derive several testable hypotheses from this logic applied to the U.S. public reaction to Security Council decisions. Specifically, the effect of SC support on public support for leaders and their policies should increase as the ideological distance between the United States and pivotal members of the SC increases. Second, the effect of appealing to the SC and failing to garner support on public support for foreign policy should decrease as the as the ideological distance between the United States and pivotal members of the SC increases. The following testable hypotheses make these claims explicit:

Hypothesis 1: All else being equal, IO support will increase public support for foreign policy.

Hypothesis 2: The effect of IO support on public support for foreign policy increases as the ideological distance between the United States and the pivotal member of a given IO increases.

Hypothesis 3: The effect of the absence of IO support on public support for foreign policy decreases as the ideological distance between the United States and pivotal member of a given IO increases.

These hypotheses are untested in empirical research on either IOs or public attitudes toward foreign policy. Importantly, they go beyond the well-documented finding that the public generally prefers multilateralism to examine how politics within security organizations affects the public's view of multilateralism. All three run counter to the realist "null hypothesis" of no institutional effects on attitudes (apart from the possible burden-sharing benefits), and hypotheses 2 and 3, in particular, distinguish the strategic information perspective from the pure legitimacy or procedural legitimacy views, as well as from the realist.[3]

---

3. Kull and Destler 1999; Eichenberg 2005; Grieco 2003.

PUBLIC SUPPORT FOR MULTILATERALISM

A general preference amongst the U.S. public for working through institutions is born out in recent research that suggests that international institutions in general and the UN in particular are held in high regard.[4] Strong majorities in the U.S. support operating through the UN; support for hypothesized uses of force increases when mentioned in conjunction with authorization from the UN.[5] This general preference supports the idea that IO authorization is valuable because it provides information that is helpful for making political decisions. But it is also consistent with the alternative view, that authorization is seen as symbolically important, regardless of whether it conveys policy-relevant information.

One way of distinguishing these perspectives is to consider variation in public reactions to institutional decisions, both across institutions and across time. For instance, public support is consistently higher for working through the UN as opposed to NATO, which supports the claim that institutional preferences affect how institutions are perceived.[6] The UNSC is likely considered more conservative with its authorization for U.S. initiatives, given its multiple vetoing members with heterogeneous preferences, although perceptions of NATO's willingness to support the United States may vary across issues. UNSC authorization appeared to boost public support prior to the first Gulf War.[7] The administration also actively publicized the authorization, suggesting recognition of the potential political boost it could provide. For instance, President George H. W. Bush appeared for a press conference in the White House Rose Garden on December 17, 1990, with ambassadors from most of the coalition countries, to note the widespread agreement and to publicize the SC resolution. In his January 16 television address from the Oval Office, the president also noted the significance of support from the UNSC and the Arab League. More recently, there is some evidence that UNSC endorsement contributed to the already high post-9/11 support for invading Afghanistan. Taken together, these facts

4. Grieco 2003; Eichenberg 2005; Kull and Destler 1999.
5. Kull and Destler 1999; Chapman and Reiter 2004.
6. For instance, A 2000 Program on International Policy Attitudes (PIPA) poll found 53 percent preferred the United States to act as part of a UN operation while only 28 percent preferred NATO. See also Thompson 2006.
7. Mueller 1994, 32. In November 1990, prior to Resolution 678, only 37 percent supported war if the Gulf situation did not change by January. After the November 29 resolution, this number rose to 53 percent. Mueller also reports questions asking about general support for the war received 10 percent higher levels when the UN vote was mentioned.

illustrate that UN decisions generally seem important to the U.S. public and that approval is valued.

Given these trends, why did opposition from France, Russia, China, and Germany (three vetoing members of the UNSC and two traditional allies), beginning in the late fall of 2002 and continuing after the onset of the war, not discourage initial public support for the war? The results of Gallup poll questions asked as late as March 2003 suggested that support for the war would drop dramatically if the United States did not consult the institution.[8] Strong majorities, as high as 65 percent in some polls, indicated that the United States should only go to war if it obtained UNSC authorization. Yet President George W. Bush received a 13 percent increase in approval ratings following the onset of hostilities in March 2003, even without a second resolution authorizing the war.[9] Put differently, the public appeared to view UNSC sanction as critically important but failure to obtain it did not diminish public support.[10] If large portions of the public viewed acting explicitly through the SC as important, why did majorities support the war without this authorization?

The strategic information perspective offers several answers to this puzzle. First, the informational perspective suggests that failure to obtain authorization from a conservative institution is unlikely to affect public opinion, as it is a "noisy" signal about the merits of proposed policies. In early 2003, the SC was likely seen as such. The most vocal opposition to the U.S. Iraq policy probably came from France, a vetoing member of the SC, including French foreign minister Dominque de Villepin's January 20 declaration that "Nothing! Nothing!" justified war.[11] Also, media pundits pointed out that both France and Russia may have had economic incentives to oppose the invasion. The public thus likely viewed the failure to obtain an SC endorsement as very noisy.

---

8. Seventy-eight percent of respondents indicated support if the SC voted for a resolution; 54 percent indicated support if the SC voted down a resolution, and only 47 percent indicated support if the United States chose not to submit a resolution at all (see the Gallup/CNN/*USA Today* poll of March 2003: USGALLUP.03MAR14.R14A-C. (Unless otherwise noted, poll data are from the Roper Center and can be found at http://roperweb.ropercenter.uconn.edu/. The call numbers given are Roper reference numbers.)

9. As late as February 2003, 56 percent of respondents said it was "necessary" to receive UN approval before an invasion of Iraq, according to a PIPA–Knowledge Networks poll. See also the *Los Angeles Times* poll of February 4, 2003, and Pew Center poll of February 20, 2003. Malone (2004, 639) provides some discussion. Various polls established strong support for the war after it began (see the Pew Research Center press release, April 10, 2003).

10. See January 2003 (USLAT.020403.R47) and February 2003 (USLAT.020903.R10) *Los Angeles Times* polls and the PIPA poll of December 3, 2002.

11. Woodward 2004, 285; see also Marfleet and Miller 2005. This point draws on Chapman 2007.

Second, strategic information models commonly find that the relationship between the principal, in this case the public, and the agent, in this case the president, moderates the effect of third-party signals. If the principal believes its agent holds preferences very close to its own, a noisy signal may have little effect on confidence in the agent. President Bush enjoyed moderately high approval ratings in the months prior to the war (between 58 percent and 64 percent in mid-March 2003), suggesting some alignment between the public's preferences and its leadership's.[12] The perception of similar preferences may have made the noisy signal of SC opposition even less likely to affect the public.

Third, Voeten's view (2005) suggests that authorization is important (and, by extension, opposition) because it signals something about the likely response of the international community. However, the signal of consequences against a powerful state may often lack credibility, in that many states in the international system derive benefits from cooperating with the United States, which limits incentives to impose costs in response to unilateral U.S. activity.[13] When member states cannot "credibly threaten" to obstruct policy, a signal of opposition is likely to be discounted by the public. In 2003, none of the P-5 were likely to implement direct opposition to U.S. action, although their lack of support may have raised the costs of the occupation and reconstruction effort. On the other hand, members still chose to voice opposition and threaten to veto because they faced domestic political opposition to the invasion. This tension helps demonstrates the trade-off in the ability of security institutions to influence public opinion—those most poised to communicate the merits of policy with their authorization may be those that are least effective at influencing public opinion through their opposition.

Of course, the surge in approval may have been due to simple patriotism following the onset of the war.[14] Others have found that the presence of war is perhaps the strongest predictor of the "rally 'round the flag" phenomena, or the change in approval surrounding the onset of military hostilities.[15] However, the anecdotal polling surrounding the Iraq War and the general public preference for working through the UN (over other institutions) is consistent with an informational perspective of security institutions. The

12. A Gallup poll conducted March 14–15, 2003, showed 58 percent approval; a CBS poll on March 17 showed 64 percent approval.
13. Brooks and Wolhforth 2005.
14. Brody 1991.
15. Chapman and Reiter 2004.

public should prefer policies that receive explicit authorization from relatively conservative institutions. Institutions with a more homogenous membership are less able to provide legitimacy through their support. Although there has not been systemic evidence gathered on public opinion regarding the membership and decision-making rules of these institutions, at least one 1994 poll found a strong majority of U.S. respondents (73 percent) indicating a desire to keep the veto system in the SC despite its anti-majoritarian nature.[16] This desire would be consistent with the informational view, as the veto system allows for biased preference outliers to convey policy-relevant information to audiences precisely because the most conservative vetoing member must support a policy in order for authorization to occur.[17]

Polls prior to the 2003 war also suggest that the public, although desiring a second UN authorization, may have been predisposed to view the Bush administration's action favorably due prior UNSC decisions. In a late-February 2003 poll 68 percent of respondents found convincing the argument that Resolution 1441, which promised "severe consequences" if Iraq did not comply with previous resolutions on weapons inspections, provided the necessary approval for war. Thus, the public may have been convinced that institutional support had already been proffered. However, in light of the publicity surrounding the administration's efforts to secure a resolution firmly authorizing an invasion, such as the wall-to-wall media coverage afforded Colin Powell's infamous "smoking gun" speech to the UN, this explanation seems questionable.

Finally, one common realist explanation for a public preference for institutional multilateralism is that the public is sensitive to the costs of foreign policy and has a preference for burden-sharing. In other words, it is not authorization that matters, but the attendant lowering of costs through the acquisition of allies that influences public opinion. Given the limitations of polling data, it is difficult to determine the relative weight of these factors. However, if the public prefers to work through institutions in order to facilitate burden-sharing, researchers should observe no difference in support for unauthorized actions undertaken with some allies and those that receive the procedural authorization of a security institution. Yet differences are often observed. For instance, prior to the 2003 Iraq War, the percentage of

16. Americans Talk Issues #25 (June 1994), USGREEN.ATI25.RB50. Forty percent responded that the veto should continue as is, while 33 percent suggested reducing veto power somewhat but keeping the system.

17. Thompson (2006), building on Gilligan and Krehbiel's conclusions about committee heterogeneity (1990), uses this logic to explain why the SC can be effective at signaling benign intent.

respondents stating that they would support the war with only a few allies was much lower when compared to war with UNSC authorization. During the Kosovo conflict, one poll showed that a full 78 percent of the public were "concerned" that the SC had not authorized the campaign, even though it was conducted under NATO auspices. Chapman and Reiter (2004) present more systematic evidence, finding that rallies 'round the flag in the United States from 1946 to 2002 were consistently larger when the SC offered a supportive resolution, while the support of regional organizations or additional allies did not significantly affect the magnitude of rallies. The strategic information perspective suggests a causal argument for why large majorities of the American public prefer the United States to act through international organizations: doing so provides information about likely foreign policy outcomes due to the institution's role as a forum for bargaining amongst member states.

RESEARCH DESIGN

This section presents a quantitative test of the above hypotheses. Ideally, one would be able to compare support for foreign policy proposals across events. Unfortunately, polling questions with comparable wording across foreign policy scenarios are not available, precluding an aggregate comparison. However, scholars have often dealt with this data limitation by examining the change in presidential approval levels during times of crisis, which has been measured frequently since the 1930s. This change is also known as the "rally 'round the flag" effect, a phenomena initially noted by Mueller (1973).[18] The study of rallies, typically measured as the change in presidential approval surrounding the onset of a foreign policy event, is useful precisely because rallies are comparable across events.[19] Presidential approval is a reasonable proxy for public support for policies, particular when measured at the time of important foreign policy events, and ever since Mueller's seminal

18. See also Mueller 1970; Parker 1995; James and Rioux 1998; Oneal, Lian, and Joyner 1996; Lian and Oneal 1993; Lai and Reiter 2004; Baker and Oneal 2001; Baum 2002; Chapman and Reiter 2004.
19. Aside from comparability, the study of rallies is important, because ideas about leadership incentives rest on public responses to foreign events. For instance, diversionary theories of war (cf. Leeds and Davis 1997; Dassel and Reinhardt 1999; Richards et al. 1993; Levy 1989) are built on the notion that leaders use military conflict as a way to bolster public opinion during times of unpopularity. Theories about the foreign policy behavior of democracies rely on the claim that the public constrains leaders (Bueno de Mesquita et al. 1999, 2003; Reiter and Stam 2002; Morgan and Campbell 1991). Thus the rally phenomena bears directly on larger implications of this study: whether IOs may constrain leaders.

study of the rally effect scholars have used approval ratings to study public reaction to foreign policy events.[20]

The research design extends that of Baker and Oneal (2001) and Chapman and Reiter (2004), which look at short-term changes in public approval of the president from immediately prior to a military dispute to immediately after the onset of the dispute. Within quantitative studies of international relations, a common source of data is that on militarized interstate disputes (MIDs). An MID is "a set of interactions between or among states involving threats to use military force, displays of military force or actual uses of military force."[21] The following analysis looks at all MIDs involving the United States from 1946 to 2001 and considers Gallup presidential approval rating.

Although scholars have studied rallies in a number of ways, there is relatively little knowledge about how IO activity affects rallies. Rallies are usually small, but tend to be larger for wars, when the opposition supports the president, when elites make public statements in support of an administration, and when the UNSC offers a favorable resolution.[22] Rallies have been positive and negative, large and small. On average, they are very minor (the mean change in presidential approval around an MID among these cases is .419 percent). However, rallies have occasionally been very large, such as those following the September 11, 2001, terrorist attacks and the onset of the Afghanistan War (33 percent) and the onset of the 1991 Persian Gulf War (18 percent).

Data on IO activity surrounding disputes are drawn from newspaper sources and the crisis summary descriptions provided by the International Crisis Behavior Project.[23] Additional data on SC decisions are from the UNSC documentation page, and data on NATO and OAS activity are available from their respective Web sites.[24] *SC authorization* is coded as a dichotomous variable based on explicit resolutions that authorize the use of force. A list of this activity is included in the appendix, but such authorization is

20. The point that approval or vote preference and attitudes about policy are linked has been made extensively, perhaps first by Campbell et al. (1964). Many other studies have pointed out the importance of approval for attitudes about policy, including Brody 1991, Lee 1977, MacKuen 1983, and Sigelman and Connover 1981.
21. Gochman and Maoz 1984, 587; Jones, Bremer, and Singer 1996.
22. Baker and Oneal 2001; Chapman and Reiter 2004.
23. Available at http://www.cidcm.umd.edu/icb/dataviewer/. Although there are more MIDs during this period than crises, most MIDs occurred during a crisis and the summary data provides information on the activity of states and IOs.
24. http://www.un.org/Docs/sc/unsc_resolutions.html; http://www.oas.org/ main/main.aspsLang= E&sLink=http://www.oas.org/documents/eng/documents.asp; http://www.nato.int/. Actual resolutions from the OAS Permanent Council and General Assembly are available electronically for only limited years. Information on NATO North Atlantic Council resolutions is available electronically through descriptions of current and past missions.

rare, occurring only six times in this sample. The clearest cases are the 1991 Gulf War, the 1950 Korean War resolution, the 1994 Haiti resolution, and the 2001 resolution authorizing an American response to the September 11 attacks and condemning the harboring of the Taliban. The other cases are a resolution in 1992 to authorize the policing of no-fly zones in Iraq and a 1992 resolution authorizing peacekeeping involving U.S. troops in the Yugoslav Civil War.[25] However, the United States formally submitted a resolution asking the council to discuss an issue or convened the council to discuss an international dispute fourteen times during the period under study. These cases did not always produce a UNSC resolution. In some instances, like during the Cuban Missile Crisis, the United States convened the SC to discuss the situation, but a formal resolution was prevented by the opposing positions of the Soviet Union and the United States.

The record for regional organization activity is similar; a regional organization participated in or authorized the use of force in only six instances. The United States has rarely appealed to these organizations for support. As examples, the United States garnered regional organization support prior to the 1999 Kosovo intervention and the 1965 intervention in the Dominican Republic, although the Dominican Republic intervention is not included in the MID dispute dataset. In the other six cases, the OAS, NATO, or SEATO backed the United States through a resolution or public statement, but there is not clear enough evidence to code these instances as formal appeals in which the United States publicly asked for organization support or authorization for action. In several cases members of a regional organization did contribute troops under regional organization auspices to U.S. efforts. In the 1962 Pathet Lao episode, for instance, SEATO troops were moved to the border of Thailand at Thailand's request. During the 1961 Berlin Wall crisis, NATO troops were stationed in West Berlin and NATO publicly backed the U.S. position. In the 1955 Costa Rica and Nicaragua dispute, the OAS convened at Costa Rica's request and an OAS fact-finding mission found Nicaragua at fault in the dispute, prompting the United States to send military aid. Prior to the 1983 U.S. invasion of Grenada, CARICOM authorized sanctions against Grenada and asked for U.S. intervention. The other two disputes coded as having regional organization involvement are NATO operations in

---

25. See Roberts 2004. The operational definition employed here is more inclusive than the legal definition, by which authorization occurred only twice (Korean War and Persian Gulf War). However, since MIDs involve many deployments of military forces short of war, the operational definition for this study includes cases in which the SC formally approved such deployments, hence the inclusion of peacekeeping and no-fly zone cases.

Kosovo and NATO participation in the 2001 Afghanistan War. In the following analysis, I include a measure of whether members of a regional organization participated with the United States under organizational auspices, although I focus primarily on SC appeals and decisions, as these have occurred with more frequency and exhibit more variance in their effects on rallies.

To examine the conditional hypothesis that public support in lieu of multilateral authorization is likely dependant on the predisposition of the organization granting support, I include a measure of the similarity of preferences between the United States and the UNSC in a given year. This measure, which was also employed in chapter 3, ranges from −1 (most distant) to 1 (most similar).[26] With China and Russia holding vetoes in the council, one might think that there would be little variance throughout the sample, particularly during the cold war. In practice, however, this measure varies from −1 in 1951 and 2003, to .009 in 1972. The empirical prediction for these years would be that the United States was most likely to try to acquire SC support in 1951 and 2003 and was least likely to attempt to acquire SC support during the 1970s, although the threat of a Soviet veto during this time may have made the potential informational benefit of SC authorization essentially irrelevant. In other words, even though authorization was quite rare during the cold war, this period provides important information for the larger study precisely because hypothesis 3 predicts that the failure to obtain authorization when it is expected to be difficult will not diminish rallies. Since the Soviet veto posed a large obstacle to the passage of United States sponsored resolutions during the cold war, the theoretical expectation would be that rallies during this period in which the United States consulted the SC will be no different than those in which the United States did not approach the council. Note that this is a different expectation than the procedural legitimacy view, which would predict larger rallies in instances in which the United States consulted the council—the "procedurally appropriate" course of action.[27]

---

26. I weight the votes equally because I have no theoretical expectations that would lead to an alternative weighting scheme. For instance, one could weight votes by their issue area or by a measure of the importance of the countries addressed by the votes. If it were possible to identify a scheme for classifying "important" votes, it would of course improve the reliability of this measure. However, there is no reason to believe that the current measure is systematically biased in any specific direction; as such the measure may be subject to more "noise" in voting patterns but not biased toward producing any particularly finding. Also, dimensionality studies have found that one dimension adequately describes voting in the SC (Voeten 2000, 2004).

27. I do not assume that the public is attentive to each vote in the UN General Assembly and then calculates the S score for each year in order to reach a conclusion about what IO support means. I do assume, however, that S is the best reasonable approximation of the distance between states'

I test hypothesis 2 by interacting the S score with *SC authorization.* I test hypothesis 3 by including the original similarity score. The joint interpretation of the interaction and original terms allows a comparison of cases of support and no support conditional on similarity to the pivotal member of the council.

As noted above, an alternative realist argument is that organizational activity might strengthen rallies because of burden-sharing. The support of an international organization signals to the public that the United States will likely receive allied support, making a rally more likely. Although the informational account and an alternative burden-sharing account may be difficult to separate empirically, I attempt to do so by controlling for the *number of allies on the side of the United States* in a dispute. As a robustness check, I substitute measures for the *number of major power allies* and measures of the *aggregate and average national capability scores of allies.* These measures did not change the substantive results. Therefore, I report the models with the simpler count of allies.

The other control variables follow Chapman and Reiter (2004) and Baker and Oneal (2001). First, I control for characteristics of the dispute that might influence public opinion. These characteristics include the *hostility level* of the MID (ranging from 1 to 5), and the *severity* of the conflict, which is an index composed of the number of actors in a dispute, the extent of great power involvement, the salience of the issues at stake, the level of violence during the crisis, and the heterogeneity of the actors in terms of military, economic, and cultural differences.[28] I also control for whether the United States was an *originator* of the dispute and if the aim of the use of force was to alter the international environment to further vital national interests (*revisionist*), which are jointly thought to be an indicator that the public will be more likely to support foreign policy actions because it perceives the United States to be protecting vital interests. Such instances also involve the administration "going public," an important component of the "opinion leadership" thesis.[29] Finally, I include a dummy measure of whether the dispute was a *war,* as others have found that wars are the single largest predictor of rally

foreign policy positions, which are manifested through a variety of behaviors that are observable to the public.

28. Brecher, Wilkenfeld, and Moser 1988, 123–27.

29. Baker and Oneal 2001; Baum 2004.

size. To capture the possibility of public "war fatigue" I include a dummy measure of whether the dispute took place in the midst of an *ongoing war.*

Second, I control for domestic factors that might influence public opinion trends. Following previous literature, I include a measure of whether the *New York Times* ran stories about the dispute on the front page (2), somewhere other than the front page (1), or not at all (0), as one precondition for a public reaction to foreign events is that they are aware of it.[30] I also control for whether the *opposition party* supported the administration (1), was neutral (0), or publicly opposed administration proposals (−1). The opposition may play an important role in opinion leadership,[31] and moreover may play a similar informational role as international organizations. In fact, the public may take opposition statements of support as particularly informative because the opposition faces incentives to point out the flaws of administration policies.[32] Related to the opinion leadership hypothesis, *official statements* by the president or high-ranking members of the administration may influence public support. I therefore include a dichotomous variable indicating whether the president or administration officials made official public statements regarding the dispute.

Finally, to control for the economic and electoral climates at the time of a dispute, I include the public's *confidence in business* over the next twelve months[33] and a measure of the number months until the *next election.* I also include the *prior level of public approval* of the president because rallies will likely be smaller when approval is already high. In other words, the inclusion of this variable corrects for bias that might be introduced because of the fact that unpopular presidents have room for major improvement.

RESULTS

The analysis is performed with a variation of a standard regression estimation, which allows one to determine the size of correlation between rallies and important events surrounding military disputes.[34] First consider

30. Aldrich, Sullivan, and Borgida 1989; Zaller 1992; Baum 2002.
31. Baker and Oneal 2001; Colaresi 2007.
32. Schultz 1999, 2001a.
33. Available at http://www.sca.isr.umich.edu/.
34. The analysis is performed with a truncated regression estimator. This procedure generates results similar to ordinary least squares (OLS) but is a more appropriate estimation technique given the censored range of the dependent variable. See Amemiya 1973; Tobin 1958. The standard errors are estimated as robust standard errors clustered by presidential administration to control for unobserved heterogeneity in approval trends across presidents.

TABLE 4.1   Determinants of rallies, 1946–2001

VARIABLE	MODEL 1: FULL SAMPLE
Prior popularity	−0.140* (0.036)
Bipartisan support	1.268 (0.907)
Administration statement	1.432* (0.397)
Next election	0.028 (0.045)
New York Times	−0.359 (0.324)
Business confidence	0.037* (0.010)
Revisionist*originator	1.397** (0.644)
War	12.153** (6.120)
Major power opposition	−1.070† (0.608)
Number of allies	−0.186† (0.106)
Ongoing war	−1.392 (0.982)
SC authorization	−119.201** (60.768)
SC authorization*S	−250.970** (125.056)
S	−2.442 (2.352)
SC consultation	−0.378 (2.165)
Regional organization activity	−0.869 (2.116)
Severity	0.909 (0.798)
Hostility level	0.121 (0.510)
Intercept	1.172 (2.514)
N	194

Note: Data are coefficient (standard error).
*Significance level: 1%.
**Significance level: 5%.
†Significance level: 10%.

table 4.1. The data support hypotheses 1 and 2, in that IO support increases rallies and that this effect decreases dramatically as the ideological similarity between the IO and the United States decreases. The coefficients on the interaction term and its components cannot be interpreted independently.[35] The coefficient for UN authorization should be interpreted as the effect of UN authorization when the S score is equal to 0. In other words, the predicted rally when the S score is equal to 0 is much smaller than the mean. This supports hypothesis, as the logic of strategic information transmission

35. See Braumoeller 2004 and Brambor, Clark, and Golder 2006.

suggests that authorization is uninformative as the S score reaches o, close the maximum value in this sample.

The findings also support hypothesis 3—that the failure to obtain multilateral approval has a much smaller effect on rally size as the ideological similarity between the IO and the proposing state decreases. The coefficient for the S variable should be interpreted as the effect of the S score when the United States does not obtain UN authorization (either because the UN was not approached or the UN was approached and the United States failed to obtain authorization). When the United States does not obtain UN authorization, an increase from −1 to o in the similarity score (roughly from the minimum to the maximum in this sample) decreases rallies by about two points, but the effect is statistically insignificant. This lack of significance is predicted; the strategic information perspective suggests that failure to obtain authorization should only affect rallies if the similarity score is positive. When the S score is less than o, the informational perspective predicts no effect of a failure to obtain authorization, and thus a coefficient that is statistically indistinguishable from o.

What about the joint effect of authorization and similarity? The interaction term shows a strong negative and statistically significant coefficient; suggesting that when UN authorization occurs and the interaction term is "switched on," positive movement in the similarity score (toward more similar) reduces rallies. Rallies with UN authorization are only larger than average when the pivotal member is ideologically distant from the United States This provides strong support for the informational rationale for IO legitimacy. Figure 4.1 displays the marginal effect of UNSC authorization at various levels of affinity (S score) with the SC.[36] Clearly, the effect of authorization on rallies decreases as similarity increases: foreign policy actions that receive authorization from a less conservative institution receive similar rallies to those that do not receive authorization from an IO.[37]

Notably, simply appealing to or consulting the SC has no discernable effect on rally size independent of receiving support. This is consistent with

36. Since the point estimates and statistical significance of the coefficients do not change when using OLS, truncated regression, clustered or normal standard errors, figure 4.1 is based on the more efficient OLS specification with robust standard errors.
37. Note that the graph suggests rallies of greater than 100 percent change in approval with authorization and an S score close to −1. However, authorization only occurs in the sample when the S score is between −.6 and −.4, meaning that predictions outside this interval are made with less confidence. This is a drawback of generating predictions based on the small number of authorizations. A more realistic interpretation would suggest that authorization should exhibit decreasing marginal returns at extreme values of S.

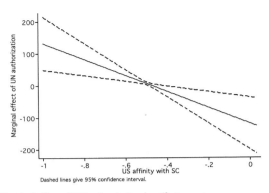

Dashed lines give 95% confidence interval.

FIGURE 4.1   Marginal effect of UN authorization by affinity

the informational perspective, as appeals without receiving support may be discounted. However, this finding is potentially at odds with the claim that public support increases when leaders simply follow procedural appropriateness. Rather, the signal and the ideological preference of the forum appear to each be important determinants of how the public will respond. The public also does not seem punish the president for not seeking multilateral approval, as there is no discernable difference in rallies in which the SC was consulted and those in which it was not. Finally, these findings seem to be at odds with claims that neutrality is always a desirable property for IOs. If public support of the president during military disputes is a valid indicator of whether the public views a particular policy is seen as worth supporting, then these findings suggest that public support is actually enhanced by approval from a more biased SC.

The other control variables mostly perform as expected. Prior popularity reduces the size of rallies. Bipartisan support slightly increases rallies, as does an official administration statement and greater consumer business confidence. Wars and disputes in which the United States was the originator and had revisionist aims received larger rallies. Major power opposition tended to reduce rallies, consistent with a view of the public as preferring low cost disputes. Interestingly, however, a greater number of allies tended to slightly reduce rally sizes, which contradicts the burden sharing hypothesis. This effect is not strong but is statistically significant.

ADDITIONAL TESTS

Although the data support hypotheses 1–3, there are several limitations to the analysis. First, it is possible that the role of the SC as well as public perceptions of it have changed since the end of the cold war. Several scholars have suggested that the organization gained legitimacy after 1990, and particularly after the successful authorization of the 1991 Persian Gulf War.[38] The basic argument is that the SC became more active in the post–cold war period because the superpower-induced deadlock that characterized earlier periods was alleviated, and citizens afforded it more legitimacy in the aftermath of this stalemate. To address the concern that the small number of post–cold war authorizations drives the results, model 2 in table 4.2 displays estimates restricted the cold war sample only. The variable SC authorization and its interaction with the S score is dropped from the model when estimated on only the cold war cases because there is only one instance of a clear authorization—the Korean War. However, the S score has a highly significant and negative coefficient in this sample (-4.431; $p < .05$), indicating that as the S score became more positive—indicating greater preference similarity between the United States and SC—the absence of authorization tended to decrease rallies during this period. This is exactly what the informational argument predicts: when a government fails to obtain authorization from an organization that is closer in its preferences, it raises questions about the how appropriate a foreign policy action is. As S increases, the failure to get external approval from the SC should raise a flag of caution with the public, while failure to get approval should have less effect as S becomes more negative.

A second concern is that given the small number of authorizations in this data, the findings may be driven by several outliers. Table 4.1 displays the distribution of rallies, with the post–September 11/Afghanistan War rally clearly an extreme outlier. Model 3 in table 4.2 displays the estimation when this outlier—the post-9/11 rally—is excluded from the analysis. The results are robust to excluding this case.[39]

Notably, the two largest rallies—the 33-point September 11 rally and the 18-point Persian Gulf War rally—occurred when the council was relatively distance ideologically from the United States, with S scores of $-.52$ in 1991 and $-.51$ in 2001, which supports the informational hypothesis. The theoretical appropriateness of excluding the outliers may therefore be questionable. These cases likely contain important information for testing the central argument—that rallies are largest when authorization occurs only if the SC is viewed as relatively distant.

38. Malone 2004; Voeten 2005.
39. In fact, the results remain unchanged to excluding any one of the six authorizations in the sample.

TABLE 4.2   Robustness tests

VARIABLE	MODEL 2: COLD WAR SAMPLE	MODEL 3: POST-9/11 EXCLUDED	MODEL 4: HIGH HOSTILITY LEVEL MIDS
Prior popularity	−.128* (0.033)	−0.130* (0.035)	−0.146* (0.031)
Bipartisan support	0.691 (1.040)	1.326 (0.871)	1.183 (0.822)
Administration statement	1.916* (.261)	1.708* (0.348)	1.555* (0.381)
Next Election	−0.584** (0.035)	0.017 (0.044)	0.043 (0.038)
New York Times	−.560† (.253)	−0.489 (0.320)	−0.400 (0.309)
Business confidence	−0.028† (0.012)	0.034* (0.010)	−0.036* (0.010)
Revisionist*originator	1.570* (0.447)	1.107 (0.673)	1.585* (0.574)
War	12.080* (4.095)	7.137** (3.814)	11.344** (6.234)
Major power opposition	−1.341** (.796)	−1.062** (0.591)	−0.796 (.680)
Number of allies	−0.650† (0.265)	−0.119** (0.062)	−0.165 (0.123)
Ongoing war	−1.156 (.799)	−1.245 (0.932)	−1.521** (0.911)
SC authorization	—	−67.700† (31.840)	−121.874† (57.034)
SC authorization*S	—	−145.000† (61.281)	−255.279† (118.116)
S	−2.614† (2.227)	−2.343	−2.774 (2.350)
SC consultation	−1.738 (3.405)	−0.970 (2.211)	−.303 (2.122)
Regional organization activity	1.884 (1.463)	−0.728 (1.976)	−0.898 (2.161)
Severity	1.326 (1.019)	0.876 (0.768)	0.912 (0.825)
Hostility level	1.015 (0.511)	0.075 (0.504)	0.910** (0.473)
Intercept	3.452 (5.181)	1.378 (2.605)	−2.025 (2.458)
N	44	193	182

Note: Data are coefficient (standard error).
*Significance level: 1%.
**Significance level: 10%.
†Significance level: 5%.

Finally, one might wonder if pooling all MIDs is appropriate, given that the public reaction to very minor disputes is likely to be muted. I therefore reran the estimation excluding MIDs with of the lowest two hostility levels, which involve only threats to use force and minor displays of force. Model 4 in table 4.2 displays the results of this analysis. The coefficients for UN authorization and the interaction term are similar in size and significance to the coefficients estimated for the full sample. The elimination of minor disputes does not dampen the results.

EXPLORATORY EXPERIMENTAL ANALYSIS

Although the results in this chapter provide important support for the informational account of IO influence, the strength of inference we can make about is somewhat limited. First, clear authorization from an international organization is rare—occurring only six times in the sample. There may also be good reason to believe that the sample may systematically exclude some outcomes of interest to the theory, such as opposition from a "friendly" organization. According to the theory, leaders should avoid such opposition, although it would be useful to know whether it would actually provoke public opposition. Second, although the similarity score employed in these tests appears to be a good proxy for audience beliefs, we cannot directly observe these or manipulate them in ways that would help provide empirical leverage for the theory. This measure is, at best, an approximation of the public's perception of the Security Council at any given point in time.

One way to address these problems is through experimental design. Thus, the remainder of this chapter reports on preliminary experimental evidence about how citizens respond to signals from potentially biased international organizations.[40] This evidence has the benefit of providing a clearer picture of causation, since many potential confounding factors are controlled for through randomization. The trade-off with any experimental design is, of course, between internal validity, in the sense of an increased ability to demonstrate causation through experimental manipulation, and external validity, or the generalizability to contexts outside of the experimental setting. To the extent that the results are consistent with the ability of citizens to respond to the bias of information sources, we can add to our confidence that the causal mechanisms proposed in chapter 2 may be at play in the real world.

This design employed here embedded an experiment in an internet survey and administered it to 268 University of Texas undergraduates. The experiment consisted of two core manipulations. First, each respondent was treated with one of two fictional news stories about the UNSC's historical relations with the United States. In one news story, the UNSC was depicted as historically restrictive in its authorization of United States initiatives,

---

40. This reports on data gathered in a collaborative project with Stephen Jessee, assistant professor at the University of Texas. I thank Stephen for allowing me to share these preliminary findings in this book.

while the other it was depicted as historically permissive. The text of the stories is listed below.

· Pro-U.S. UN priming: "The United Nations Security Council convened last Wednesday to discuss several important security issues in the world. The Security Council has a solid record of supporting U.S. initiatives in all areas of the globe and experts expect the council to develop a resolution heavily influenced by U.S. goals. Since its inception in 1945, the Security Council has only failed to adopt resolutions put forth by the United States twice, while passing over 400 U.S. initiatives. Despite several high-profile debates in the council, it has historically been regarded as an advocate of U.S. policy and, since the United States holds an important position on the council, its policy has traditionally been dictated by U.S. interests. Those close to current debates expect that this discussion about security initiatives will proceed along similar lines."

· Anti-U.S. UN priming: "The United Nations Security Council convened last Wednesday to discuss several important security issues in the world. The Security Council has historically played an important role as a counter to U.S. dominance in most areas of the globe. Since its inception in 1945, the Security Council has only passed resolutions put forth by the United States twice, while voting down over 400 U.S. initiatives. The council also has historically been extremely conservative in granting authorization for various military actions. The United States, in particular, has had difficulty garnering Council support because many of its members often oppose U.S. policy and unipolarity. Those close to current debates expect that this discussion about security initiatives will proceed along similar lines."

Respondents were then presented with five questions about hypothetical uses of force, ranging in intensity and varying in the target. In each question we randomly manipulated whether the respondent was told that the UN Security Council supported or opposed the initiative. These two manipulations—priming regarding the UNSC bias and the signal of authorization or opposition—set up the following two-by-two experimental design, shown in table 4.3.

These treatments were randomly administered in order to control for respondent characteristics that might traditionally be associated with attitudes about the use of force, such as gender, political ideology, and age, although the latter is necessarily restricted because of the population from which we sampled respondents. Also, in order to see if attitudes might systematically be driven by the type of foreign policy proposed—for example, sanctions, humanitarian intervention, or military invasion—we asked respondents five different questions after priming them with the UN bias treatment:

· "The United Nations Security Council has voted (for/against) a resolution to authorize the United States to take preemptive actions to bomb suspected nuclear weapons development sites inside of Iran. Would you support the U.S. taking this action or not?"

TABLE 4.3   2×2 Experimental design

UN BIAS	OPPOSE	SUPPORT
Pro-U.S.	Increased opposition	Little or no change
Anti-U.S.	Little or no change	Increased support

· "American military officials claim that armed militants are hiding out in the mountainous regions along the Afghanistan-Pakistan border. The government of Pakistan is opposed to letting United States troops into their country to battle these militants. The United Nations Security Council has voted (for/against) a resolution to allow the United States to enter Pakistan to search for these groups. Would you approve of the U.S. taking this action or not?"
· "The U.S. has proposed a series of economic sanctions on Iran because the country has refused to comply with nuclear inspections. The United Nations Security Council has voted (for/against) these sanctions. Do you support these sanctions?"
· "A North Korean submarine has fired torpedoes at a Japanese ship, sinking the ship and killing many of the crew members. The United States is planning to send troops to invade North Korea. The United Nations Security Council has voted (for/against) a resolution authorizing this invasion. Would you support the United States taking this action?"
· "The United Nations Security Council has voted (for/against) a resolution to send peacekeeping troops into Darfur to combat genocide in the region. Would you support United States troops being sent as part of this mission?"

In each case respondents were given the option of strongly supporting (4), weakly supporting, weakly opposing, strongly opposing (1), or answering "don't know." For each of these scenarios, the informational perspective would suggest that respondents that receive a prompt depicting the UNSC as biased against the United States should have had higher levels of support for policies that receive UNSC support, while respondents that receive a prompt depicting the UNSC as biased in favor of the United States should have had lower levels of support for policies that receive UNSC opposition.

While the experimental design allowed for randomization across respondents, and therefore should have ruled out a number of confounding variables, this would not be the case if potential confounders are not themselves randomly distributed across our sample. That is, if the sample was overwhelmingly comprised of individuals of a certain type, then we have reduced ability to control for the effects of that type on attitudes. Due to

TABLE 4.4   Average support of Iraq troops pooled across scenarios

UN PROMPT	OPPOSE	SUPPORT
Anti-U.S. Council	1.72	2.16
Pro-U.S. Council	1.66	2.21

Note: The entries are the average level of support across four category answers where 1 = strongly oppose, 2 = oppose, 3 = support, and 4 = strongly support.

several potential confounders, therefore, these results should be regarded as preliminary. First, the sample was one of opportunity, in that it was comprised of mostly freshman and sophomore students at a flagship state university. Thus, there was limited age variation in our sample. Second, one might naturally expect political knowledge about foreign affairs to moderate the power of our "treatment." That is, if individuals knew a lot about the UN the treatment may have little effect.

To assess this latter concern, respondents were asked a battery of factual questions about foreign affairs ranging from contemporary history to geography to basic facts about other countries and international organizations. Respondents were also asked to identify the five permanent members of the UN Security Council. Out of 268 respondents, 78 (29 percent) correctly identified all five permanent members, while another 82 (31 percent) correctly identified four of the five. These questions were then combined into several scales: one in which we simply summed the number of correct answers to these factual questions and the number of correctly identified P-5, and a similar scale in which only correctly identifying all of the P-5 counted as a correct answer. The level of foreign affairs knowledge in the sample is relatively slightly right skewed, which means that our respondents were fairly knowledgeable. This preliminary sample is also relatively small, with only 258 respondents. While this is certainly adequate for basic inference, it limits the power to conduct more sophisticated conditional explorations.

Table 4.4 shows mean levels of support across all five hypothetical foreign policy scenarios. The results clearly show a main effect for UN Security Council support on respondents' average support for various foreign policy scenarios. However, the findings are more mixed with respect to the conditional effect of the UN bias priming on the effect of support or opposition. There is not substantial variation in average support levels from respondents that saw support from the UN Security Council, regardless of the prompt they received about the general stance of the Security Council relative to the United States The appendix to this chapter displays results from each of the individual foreign policy scenarios, which are also mixed with respect to the conditional nature of UN authorization.

In summary, the preliminary experimental results with respect to the UN questions were only partially suggestive, as the results were consistent with both a legitimacy and information perspective. Both theoretical accounts predicted that individuals should be more likely to support foreign policies that receive support from a multilateral institution like the UN. The treatments in this case were intended to provoke a conditional moderation of the effect of support, but only if they achieved their intended goal. As an extension to the informational argument, however, the respondents were asked a series of related experiments about information provided from other political sources. For the present purposes, I only present one of these additional experiments, which had a similar design to the above questions but focused on support from then presidential candidates Barack Obama and John McCain. Specifically, respondents were asked whether they would support increasing troop levels in Iraq and manipulated whether they were told that Barack Obama or John McCain supported the use of force. In a pre-manipulation portion of the survey, respondents were also asked to place John McCain and Barack Obama on a scale of 1 to 5 indicating their willingness to use force to solve problems in the world. The mean response for Obama was 2.10 (SD ±.80), while the mean response for McCain was 4.20 (SD ±.75), suggesting that on average the respondents viewed John McCain as more hawkish than Barack Obama when it comes to using force.

Given these perceptions of the candidates, the biased-information argument would suggest that support of the use of force from Obama (McCain) would be a much more informative (noisy) signal about the need to use force in a given situation. Table 4.5 shows mean levels conditional on seeing either McCain's or Obama's stance on increasing troop levels in Iraq.

Clearly, respondents were more likely to support increased troop levels upon seeing support from the perceived "dovish" candidate—Obama—than upon seeing support from the perceived "hawkish" candidate—McCain. Respondents were also less likely to oppose increased troop levels when the

TABLE 4.5   Average support of Iraq troops increase conditional on presidential candidate

CANDIDATE	OPPOSE	SUPPORT
Obama	1.03	1.42
McCain	.90	.98

Note: The entries are the average level of support across four category answers where 1 = strongly oppose, 2 = oppose, 3 = support, and 4 = strongly support.

TABLE 4.6   Support for Iraq troop increase, by likely presidential vote

CANDIDATE	OPPOSE	SUPPORT
McCain Supporters		
Obama	.80	1.09
McCain	.63	.60
Obama Supporters		
Obama	1.81	2.28
McCain	1.23	1.77

Note: The entries are the average level of support across four category answers where 1 = strongly oppose, 2 = oppose, 3 = support, and 4 = strongly support.

"dovish" candidate—Obama—opposed it than when the hawkish candidate—McCain—opposed.

These trends were even more clear when likely McCain and Obama supporters were separated. McCain supporters placed Obama at an average level of 1.69 on the willingness to use force scale, compared to an average of 2.10 in the entire sample, while Obama supporters placed McCain at an average level of 4.36, compared to an average of 4.20 in the entire sample. That is, McCain supporters were more likely to believe Obama is a dove than the average respondent, while Obama supporters were more likely to believe that McCain is a hawk than the average respondent. Given these priors, table 4.6 shows average respondent support levels broken down by likely McCain voters and likely Obama voters.

The key take-home point from these tables is that amongst McCain supporters, respondents were much more likely to support an Iraq troop increase when they were told that Obama supported it than when they were told McCain supported it. In other words, the biased-information effect seems to trump the partisan id effect of supporting initiatives supported by candidates one likes.[41]

DISCUSSION AND CONCLUSION

Despite the traditional view of multilateral security institutions as "toothless," recent work and the theory in chapter 2 suggests that SC decisions matter either because they signal vital information about policies to key audi-

41. See Schultz 2005 for a theory addressing this issue.

ences or they posses important symbolic legitimacy. However, the symbolic legitimacy and strategic information approaches suggest different empirical patterns. The symbolic legitimacy account suggests that legitimacy should be relatively fixed or slow-changing, whereas the strategic information account suggests that behavior consistent with legitimacy—such as behaving as if an institution's decisions should be trusted and followed—is likely to be conditional on observer's beliefs about the incentives of actors driving those decisions. In the context of the SC, those actors are key veto-wielding states. Thus, the reaction to SC decisions should be conditional on audiences' beliefs about the interests of those states.

This chapter presented a test of two hypotheses, based in the logic of strategic information transmission. The hypotheses predicted that the effect of SC decisions on U.S. public opinion is conditional on public perceptions of the council. The primary test of these hypotheses yielded strong support even after controlling for a range of commonly included determinants of presidential approval. This evidence remains largely even after excluding several outlying cases, focusing on only disputes of higher hostility level, and limiting analysis to the cold war subsample. These findings lend considerable support to the informational theory. The potential benefit of appealing to an unbiased institution is clear from the above evidence. On one hand, the added boost in public support dramatically increases as an institution becomes more biased against authorization. However, a public backlash is less likely to occur due to IO opposition as an institution becomes more biased. The risk-return trade-off is straightforward: it is less risky and more of a return to appeal to multilateral security IOs when they are biased against authorization.

This evidence has implications for larger theoretical debates about the influence of institutions on state behavior. The realist tradition suggests that IOs matter least in security affairs, where power politics is thought to dominate. These results suggest that security IOs can matter in an unexpected way (from the realist point of view)—by influencing public opinion, which can in turn constrain or influence leaders. This suggests that more attention should be focused on how the presence and behavior of IOs can affect statecraft through indirect channels, such as the anticipation of public reaction to IO decisions. The constructivist tradition has offered a different interpretation of the effects of IOs and legitimacy in world affairs. According to constructivists, IOs can enhance legitimacy because it is procedurally appropriate to consult IOs prior to conducting foreign policy. The analyses above, however, show that the effect of IO authorization is, in fact, conditional on public perceptions. The legitimacy effect, in other words, may vary according to the prevailing view of an IO's preferences. This is a worthwhile addition to both constructivist and rationalist ideas about institutional influence.

Finally, the evidence provides support for the strategic information approach, despite the heavy burden this places on the attention and sophistication of domestic audiences with regard to international events. In general, there is little micro-level evidence of how audiences might respond to different types of international activity, although behaviorists have traditionally found that citizens are ill-informed about the specifics of international politics. Recent experimental work goes far in addressing issue, in that experimental approaches may control stimuli in order to determine whether the average person reacts in ways predicted by many theories that involve domestic constraints.[42]

42. For example, Tomz 2007a.

APPENDIX: EXPERIMENTAL RESULTS AND CASES OF
U.S. CONSULTATION OF THE UNSC

TABLE 4A.1   UN consultations by the United States and Security Council resolutions over the period studied

DISPUTE	START DATE	UN AUTHORIZATION	RESOLUTION NUMBER
Berlin Blockade	April 1, 1948	No	NA
Korean War	June 25, 1950	Yes	38
PRC attack on Quemoy	August 27, 1954	No	NA
Sinai War*	October 30, 1956	No	NA
Cuban Missile Crisis	October 22, 1962	No	NA
Vietnam War	August 4, 1964	No	NA
Seizure of USS *Pueblo*	January 23, 1967	No	NA
October War	October 6, 1973	No	NA
Iran Hostage Crisis	November 4, 1979	No	NA
Persian Gulf War	January 16, 1991	Yes	678 (see also 677, 661–662, 664–667, 674, 677–678)
Iraq no-fly zone violations	March 5, 1991	Yes	678 (see also 677, 661–662, 664–667, 674, 677–678)
Yugoslav Civil War	November 17, 1992	Yes	781, 786, 787
Haiti invasion	October 20, 1993	Yes	940
North Korea nuclear standoff	March 13, 1993	No	NA
Iraq threatens Kuwaiti border	October 8, 1994	No	NA
Afghanistan War	September 15, 2001	Yes	1368

*Not included in analysis due to missing polling data.

TABLE 4A.2   Data from individual experimental questions

UN PROMPT	OPPOSE	SUPPORT
	Bombing Iran	
Anti-U.S. Council	**1.11**	1.18
Pro-U.S. Council	1.03	1.21
	Troops Into Pakistan Border Region	
Anti-U.S. Council	1.16	1.60
Pro-U.S. Council	1.60	1.84
	Sanctioning Iran	
Anti-U.S. Council	**1.69**	**2.30**
Pro-U.S. Council	1.55	2.17
	Invade North Korea	
Anti-U.S. Council	0.93	1.12
Pro-U.S. Council	0.95	1.36
	Darfur Peacekeepers	
Anti-U.S. Council	1.98	**2.45**
Pro-U.S. Council	1.96	2.28

Note: The entries are the average level of support across four category answers where 1 = strongly oppose, 2 = oppose, 3 = support, and 4 = strongly support.

5

INTERNATIONAL ORGANIZATIONS AND COALITION BUILDING

Aside from building support at home, do multilateral security organizations facilitate coalition building prior to military action? The idea that getting external approval will buy off allies is certainly an oft-cited reason for appealing to IOs, as examples discussed throughout this book demonstrate. One reason for this is proposed by the view of IOs as coordination devices, which suggests that institutions facilitate coalition building by providing focal solutions or by reducing transaction costs (e.g., Martin 1992; Keohane 1984). Foreign policy conducted through international organizations should elicit more cooperation, because states can more readily come to agreement on what is expected of one another. The prevalence of focal solutions may also make clearer what constitutes a transgression from agreed upon rules, providing further incentives for cooperation.

The informational theory offered in chapter 2 suggests a related but distinct causal logic. Authorization by international security organizations can provide information to relevant audiences about a proposed foreign policy action, freeing up domestic constraints for potential allies. This in turn relieves political disincentives allies may face when considering joining international disputes. This logic is more specific to security disputes than the general notion of focal points, but is related in the sense that the creation of legitimacy, through the transmission of information, may make it easier for states to cooperate on a given course of action as it alleviates domestic political incentives for defection from the agreed upon solution. For example, as mentioned in previous chapters, Tony Blair suggested prior to the 2003 Iraq War that Security Council authorization was a political necessity for his government (Woodward 2004; Gordon and Trainor 2006). Of course, the British joined the American coalition despite the failure to receive a second Security Council authorization, but Tony Blair's Labour Party suffered in the subsequent election, no doubt in part due to the unpopularity of the war. The notion that IOs, under certain conditions, can provide information that alleviates domestic constraints for potential allies suggests an alternative explanation for the coordinating role of institutions.

Apart from the case of Britain prior to the Iraq War, there is anecdotal evidence that the UN Security Council, and perhaps smaller regional organizations, play this role. Several states, including Australia, explicitly require Security Council authorization for participation in multilateral uses of force (Voeten 2005). Security Council authorization was deemed important for the domestic audiences of Arab allies prior to the 1991 Gulf War (Bush and Scowcroft 1998), and OAS support may have allowed some Caribbean nations to support the U.S. invasion of Grenada in 1983. Like states requesting authorization for action, potential allies appear to act as if multilateral approval is an important precondition for their participation in international disputes.

The informational account predicts, however, that effect of IO authorization is contingent on the ideological affinity between the authorizing organization and the state proposing a foreign policy action. When authorization comes from a more conservative source, states should be much more willing to join in multilateral uses of force. When authorization comes from a more willing institution, however, the effect of authorization should be much weaker. Similarly, when authorization is denied by an ideologically distant organization, a state may still deem it worthwhile to join in a multilateral use of force, as opposition may be discounted by the state's citizenry. Again, this intuitively appears to be the case, as Gulf states' support in the first Gulf War would likely not have been forthcoming without explicit UN Security Council sanction and Russian support, although other traditional allies of the United States were willing to support the United States military operations.

An additional consideration of an outside observer, such as a foreign citizen, is the relationship between the observer and the signaler. In general information transmission models, uninformed observers often update their beliefs according to whether their preferences are aligned with those of a more informed agent. When an audience views its preferences as similar to those of a more informed agent, it will tend to update its beliefs in tune with the signal sent by that agent, while discounting signals from agents that have opposed preferences. Applying this logic to the decision of foreign publics to support their government's intervention in a dispute, foreign citizens should be attuned to the similarity between their state and the signaler—for instance the Security Council. When the foreign audience views the preferences of a multilateral organization as similar to it and its government's own, it is more likely to defer to its government's and the organization's point of view. In other words, the relationship between a state requesting authorization and an IO as well as the relationship between that IO and foreign states should affect the likelihood of foreign states joining crisis actors in international disputes.

This chapter provides a test of the claim that the effect of organizational activity on coalition building is contingent on the ideological distance between an IO and a proposing state in a multilateral use of force, as well as the ideological distance between an IO and a potential coalition partners. The next section reviews some relevant literature on how organizations may facilitate cooperation in security affairs. I then discuss an extension to the model in chapter 2 that introduces a foreign government and foreign audience. The foreign audience is uncertain about the likely outcome of foreign policies and looks to signals of a potential aggressor and an international organization for information about whether it would be good for its own government to lend support. The model shows how organizational support can sometimes facilitate coalition building, while opposition can sometimes diminish the prospects for coalition building. The remainder of the chapter discusses empirical examples of this process and presents some findings based on statistical analyses.

INTERNATIONAL ORGANIZATIONS AND COOPERATION

Many scholars note that international organizations can help states coordinate policies through such mechanisms as commitment and information sharing (e.g., Martin 1992; Martin and Simmons 1998). With regard to security organizations in particular, coordination through an IO may force commitment to a policy choice in situations in which states might normally free ride, relying on others to enforce the policy. For instance, in applying sanctions on a state defying nuclear proliferation treaties, while it is in all states' interests to limit the proliferation of weapons, individual states stand to gain by free riding on the enforcement actions of others. Enforcement is costly in terms of suspended trade and material monitoring costs and individual states may benefit from violating the agreed upon sanction regime while enjoying the disincentive to produce nuclear weapons created by other states' costly punishment. Formal commitment in a public forum may help alleviate the tendency to free ride and thus ensure cooperation on a common sanction strategy.

The ability to coordinate on policy choices is beneficial in many areas, from trade policy to international telecommunications (Cowhey 1990). From the point of view of IOs as coordination devices, the authorization of consultative security organizations should spur others to act, thereby reducing free riding and buck passing and improving the chances of policy success. Voeten (2005) develops this logic more fully, arguing that the Security Council acts as an "elite pact," a coordination device characterized by its exclusivity. Elite pacts, according to Voeten, are very useful at assuaging fears of exploitation. In this sense, authorization from the Security Council can facilitate cooperation abroad (see also Thompson 2006).

Why would authorization from an institution help solidify cooperation of states, like Great Britain in 2003, that otherwise agree with a policy and have the material capability to contribute? Sometimes authorization is useful for loosening domestic constraints, lowering the overall costs of foreign policy (Chapman 2007; Fang 2008; Chapman and Wolford 2010). The authorization of an institution like the Security Council can alleviate the concerns of potential partners over the potential political costs of contribution to foreign policy by placating foreign public opinion and lowering the chances of broader international opposition. IO authorization can thus make it more likely that other states join with states undertaking potentially costly foreign policies.

INFORMATION PROVISION AND COALITION BUILDING

Potential "joiners" or allies may desire a revisionist state to garner some form of formal, institutional support because it signals to their own audience that a given policy is worth contributing to. However, whereas a view of IOs as general coordination devices predicts that IO involvement improves the chances of forming a successful coalition, an informational theory predicts that the ability of IOs to facilitate coalition formation is conditional on the type and credibility of signals emanating from IOs. The notion that multilateral authorization alleviates concerns abroad implies that authorization communicates important information to foreign parties. Foreign governments and citizens may seek reassurance that initiating states are not acting

FIGURE 5.1   Sequence with a foreign audience and government

overly expansionist; at the same time foreign governments may seek authorization as a means of placating their own domestic audiences. But extending the logic of chapter 2 to this process suggests that authorization may not always be equally effective at facilitating coordination, while opposition may not always diminish the chances of multilateral opposition.

Consider a slight variant of the model presented in chapter 2 in which the actors are a proposing state, the pivotal member of an IO, a potential ally state, and the domestic public in that ally state. Assume that the sequence of the game is nearly identical to that in chapter 2, with an actor proposing some policy whose consequences are uncertain from the point of view of a foreign public. The proposing actor has the option of consulting a multilateral institution for approval, after which the foreign audience decides whether they would support their government lending aid to the proposer. Finally, the foreign government decides, after taking stock of their public's opinion, whether they should ultimately lend support to the proposing state.

The foreign audience, like the domestic audience in chapter 2, may or may not have accurate perceptions about the exact location of member states' and the proposing state's ideal policy preferences. Figure 5.1 shows the sequence of the game.

Because the basic dynamics of this setup are identical to those presented in chapter 2, the following is an informal discussion of the core insights.[1] First, assume that the foreign state is attentive to public opinion; otherwise the foreign state simply chooses to support policies it prefers to the status quo and oppose others; the information provision to the foreign audience becomes irrelevant. When the foreign government is attentive to its domestic public's preferences, its decision weighs its own preferences against the cost of defying its public. It is possible that a foreign government will choose participation when its own public opposes it, but it is less likely to do so, especially if its preferences are more closely correlated with its own public than that of a foreign government.

Once we consider the foreign government to be constrained by its domestic audience, the equilibria of this game are similar to those in chapter 2.

---

1. See the theoretical appendix of this chapter for a slightly more technical discussion.

Namely, support from an organization that is more conservative than the crisis actor makes a potential intervener's support much more likely, while opposition has little effect. Again, states that desire the participation of allies will avoid the sanction of more revisionist organizations because it will strongly discourage the participation of potential allies. However, the third-party observer must consider its preference relationship with that of the proposing state, as well as the signaler, the multilateral organization. Domestic audiences are, on the whole, more likely to identify with their own state than other states, and these states may have distributive conflicts over the ultimate outcome of foreign policies. In particular, if an organization is viewed as more conservative than the proposing state, multilateral support is more likely to generate allied participation as the foreign audience's preferences conform more closely to both the organization and the proposing state. Given a signal of opposition from a conservative institution, the potential ally's participation also depends on its preference relationship to the proposing state, as it has more information about potential outcomes and hence does not rely on the signal of the institution to make a judgment about foreign policy.[2] In other words, the institution's decision operates through its effect on the audience of the foreign state, which may be able to impose some punishments or rewards upon its own government for making "good" policy choices.

If an organization is viewed as more revisionist than the proposing state, the participation of a potential ally only depends on the foreign audience's preference relationship to the crisis actor. This is because, once again, support from this type of institution does not convey a clear signal about the costliness of foreign policy, other than it is within some wide range of possible policies. If the foreign audience is hawkish and has identical preferences as the institution, then the best response to a supportive resolution is of course to support he policy. But in the more likely event that the foreign audience is rather dovish and requires reassurances about the costs of foreign policy, support from a more revisionist or hawkish institution will not enable the audience to draw strong inferences about the merits of a proposed policy and the audience must base its decision on how closely its preferences are to the proposing state. In other words, not only does the conservatism of the institution matter for outcomes, but also the degree to which the foreign audience sees its preferences aligned with the crisis actor.

2. This again assumes away the idea that the potential ally relies on IO authorization to tell them something about the likely response of important states in the system.

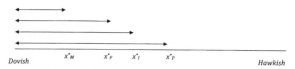

FIGURE 5.2   Policy preferences with a "dovish institution"

Consider figure 5.2, which illustrates the range of policies that each actor will sincerely support for a hypothetical preference ordering placing the proposing state as the most hawkish (P), followed by the intervener (I), the foreign public (F), and the pivotal institutional member (M).

In the figure x^*_i refers to the policy furthest from the status quo that actor i prefers to the status quo. With this preference ordering, a signal of support from a multilateral institution will cause the foreign audience to learn with certainty that the likely policy outcome falls within the range of policies it prefers to the status quo, although it is not able to determine this having simply observed the proposing state propose the policy. As long as the foreign audience is more conservative in its preference for the use of force abroad, the foreign audience's willingness to support policies plays a constraining role on its government. Even if the government strictly preferred to join with the proposing state, it may be limited by what its own public will support. The sanction of an international institution can help the audience make its decision with more information, which can alleviate domestic constraints.

RELATIVE PREFERENCES, CHEAP TALK, AND COALITION BUILDING

The introduction of a third-party audience results in several interesting and novel empirical implications. In general, the probability that a potential intervener comes to the aid of a state in crisis depends on four factors: (1) whether the state in crisis consults a multilateral organization and the decision of that organization; (2) the preference relationship between the crisis actor and the organization (3) the preference relationship between the foreign audience and the crisis actor; and (4) the preference relationship between the foreign audience and the organization.

Like domestic audiences, there is reason to believe that foreign audiences are less than perfectly informed about the preferences of crisis actors and member states of an international organization (although they may have a better estimation of their own government's preferences). Thus, the preference relationship between the foreign audience, the crisis actor, and the pivotal member of an IO is subject to some uncertainty, as was the relation-ship between the domestic audience and pivotal member in chapter 2. But subject to this uncertainty, three claims should probabilistically follow from the logic above. First, the support of a multilateral organization is more likely to result in the cooperation of allies if the organization is perceived to be more conservative relative to the proposing state. Second, the support of a multilateral organization is more likely to result in the cooperation of allies the more the interests of the ally's audience and those of the organization are perceived to coincide. Third, cooperation is more likely, regardless of organizational activity, as the interests of the ally and its public and those of the proposing state are seen to coincide.

These claims add to the insights developed in the previous chapters. If one indicator of organizational legitimacy is whether third-party actors de-fer to organizations' decisions, the informational argument points out that this is contingent how organizations are perceived, both in terms of their interests relative to a potential revisionist state and the similarity of the organizations' interests to foreign observers. This result demonstrates the common principal agent relationship that a principal with private informa-tion whose preferences converge with the agent is often optimal. From the point of view of allies, participation is much more attractive if the crisis ac-tor is pursuing goals consistent with one's own. This belief is strengthened when the crisis actor's preferences conform to the potential ally or when a multilateral organization with preferences similar to the ally's condones (op-poses) a proposed foreign policy.

PUBLIC DIPLOMACY AND COALITION BUILDING

States that need to build wide coalitional support for their foreign policies face a challenging political landscape. As several recent U.S. foreign policy initiatives show, efforts to address threats to international peace and security or to remake the international landscape frequently require active and tacit support from a variety of countries. Obtaining this cooperation can involve expending substantial political and material capital. States will often make the case that their allies have a direct stake in the outcomes of their foreign policy initiatives and will go to many lengths, including cutting material side deals, to exact cooperation.

A central component of this process is in making the case to foreign pub-lics that a proposed foreign policy will not be overly expansive and will not be too disruptive to their country's security. As George H. W. Bush and Brent

Scowcroft note in their memoirs (1998), placating Arab public opinion was a preeminent concern for both Arab governments and the United States prior to the first Gulf War and played a prominent role in the decision to garner UN Security Council approval. Likewise, previous chapters mentioned Tony Blair's concern over the domestic political costs of supporting the 2003 Iraq War, and other countries like Japan and Australia virtually require Security Council approval for participation in peacekeeping and military operations. In these and other cases the level of allied support depended critically on the decision of a multilateral security body.

Alex Thompson (2009) has developed a related logic in a well-crafted study of how powerful states channel coercion through multilateral institutions. In particular, Thompson has shown that the U.S. decision to work through the UN to deal with Iraq's weapons programs during the 1990s and in early in the new millennium was aimed at obtaining international cooperation. As Thompson points out, this is especially important when foreign publics fear exploitation, which is much more possible when a militarily and economically powerful state engages in foreign policy initiatives. Reducing those fears of exploitation is a central function of securing multilateral approval for foreign policies.

More generally, public diplomacy plays a central role in assuaging public fears of exploitation and aggression, but basic cheap-talk arguments show us that direct, bilateral diplomacy and public overtures are often only partially effective. This is because a would-be aggressor has an interest to signal that it has limited aims, even if its true aims are world domination. The presence of a third party that can serve as a public forum for discussion about proposed policies can therefore serve an important function for the rest of the world. The debate and decision of this institution can provide some additional information about the likely consequences of foreign policies, allowing foreign audiences to make better judgments as to whether their governments should play an active role in the policy implementation.

Conventional wisdom, however, might hold that in order for an institution to be useful in this regard, it must be seen as objective, neutral, or altruistic. The informational argument shows that this is not the case. In fact, by design the UN Security Council is not neutral, objective, or altruistic, as it affords veto power to countries with vested stakes in most efforts to remake international order. But by its design, its authorization can be particularly informative to foreign audiences, precisely because it is unlikely that all five veto-wielding states will authorize a policy that would have negative consequences for a significant segment of the world's population. This is not because those states have an altruistic interest in the world's population (although this impulse may exist in many circumstances), but rather because they are protecting their own interests.

Other organizations are useful in this regard as well, although their usefulness varies as a function of how closely they are aligned with the interests of a proposing country. In general, forums where it is difficult to obtain support are very useful outlets for public diplomacy aimed at foreign audiences. The same logic that applies to domestic interests applies to foreign interests: foreign audiences can infer that authorization from a body with a high "legislative hurdle" is unlikely unless the potential negative consequences of foreign policy are minimal. On the other hand, opposition can occur for a wide range of policies.

INTERNATIONAL PUBLIC OPINION

Whether opposition is seen as useful for foreign policies, however, depends additionally on how closely aligned a foreign public sees its interests relative to key countries in an international organization. For instance, Europeans and Americans reacted very differently to the failure to obtain Security Council support for the 2003 Iraq War, most likely because one of the key Security Council members opposing the war was France. Likewise, Germany, who was a rotating member at the time, had announced its opposition to the war. From the point of view of German, French, and many other continental Europeans, this was strong evidence that they should also not support the war. In other words, these citizens were more likely to view their preferences as more closely aligned with their own governments than the United States', priming public support for the war in Europe to be very low. In the counterfactual case that the United States could have obtained Security Council approval, including a yes vote from countries like France and Germany, public support for the war in Europe would likely have been much higher.

There is considerable cross-country variation in attitudes toward the United Nations and the Security Council, which supports the notion that whether or not UN Security Council resolutions are deemed important by international audiences can often depend on public perceptions of the UN. A 2007 Program on International Policy Attitudes (PIPA) study is one of the more recent attempts to gather broad, cross-national data on attitudes toward the UN.[3] Its general findings showed that on average, majorities of

3. PIPA 2007.

respondents across many countries and regions believe that the Security Council should have the authority to authorize the use of force to intervene in humanitarian crises, even when it contradicts the sovereign requests of national governments. The study also showed generally high support for allowing the United Nations to play an active role in training and deploying peacekeepers, investigating human rights violations, and regulating international arms trade, although there was less support for allowing the UN to impose supranational taxes as sanctions for countries violating their international obligations.

However, the study showed much more cross-country variation in agreement with the statement, "When dealing with international problems, [survey country] should be more willing to make decisions within the United Nations even if this means that [survey country] will sometimes have to go along with a policy that is not its first choice" (PIPA 2007, 25). Responses varied from 15 percent agreement in the Palestinian territories to 78 percent agreement in China. France and the United States showed 68 percent and 60 percent agreement, respectively, while the Philippines (26 percent), Ukraine (30 percent), and Russia (33 percent) showed lower levels of agreement with the statement.[4] These attitudes are no doubt driven by domestic political climate, culture, and other forces, but the key point is that foreign audiences vary in their general attitudes toward compliance with UN Security Council decisions. This in turn suggests that the degree to which organizational support or authorization affects coalition building may depend in large part on the prior perceptions of key audiences and their influence on their home governments.

As I noted in earlier chapters, majorities of American citizens supported the 2003 Iraq War without Security Council authorization, despite indicating before the war that such authorization would be highly valued. In other words, these citizens, in addition to responding in a patriotic fashion, appeared to discount the disapproval of several key members of the Security Council. But opposition was not discounted elsewhere. For instance, Turkish lawmakers voted against allowing the United States to use Turkish soil as a staging ground for moving across Iraq's northern border, despite providing support in the first Gulf War.[5] Such access would have provided invaluable

---

4. The percent in agreement in the United States is in accordance with Kull and Destler's claim that the majority of U.S. citizens favor engagement with the world through international institutions (1999). Notably, however, the same PIPA study (2007) showed the United States as ranking among the lowest or "coolest" countries when respondents were asked to rate the UN according to a feeling thermometer, perhaps due to lingering resentment about the lack of support for the Iraq War.

5. See Nye 2003 and Rubin 2003 on the perceived lack of legitimacy for the Iraq War in Turkey.

strategic and tactical benefits to the U.S. effort, but was not forthcoming due to concerns over the lack of multilateral support for the war. Turkish citizens and lawmakers seemed to view their preferences as more closely allied with their allies in Western Europe who opposed the war rather than their NATO allies, the United States and Great Britain. Similar reactions were well-documented in Western Europe, illustrating the importance of perceived preference alignment.[6]

Aside from anecdotal evidence about cross country and cross-institutional variation in the coalition building effects of multilateral institutions, we can also look at broader aggregate trends. In particular, we would like to know whether (a) coalition building is more likely when a proposing state consults and wins the approval of a multilateral institution and (b) whether the effect of institutional support or opposition is conditional on the relative preference distance between potential allies and an international institution.

Designing a statistical test to examine this is nontrivial, however. First, one cannot simply observe successful cases of coalition building, as there may be many unsuccessful cases in which only one or a few allies joined in the cause of a proposing state. Moreover, there may be cases in which a proposing state chooses to moderate initial aims because its government anticipates being unable to successfully garner allied support. For these reasons, I use the basic dataset employed in chapter 3 containing data on international crises. These include international crises at varying levels of intensity and are a good starting point for considering opportunities for multilateral consultation and coalition building.

Second, it is not immediately clear which states should be included in the sample of potential interveners or allies. One possibility would be to examine the alliance relationships of each country in a given time period and code all alliance partners as potential coalition partners. However, we know that many informal coalitions have included states that do not share a formal alliance. As an alternative we can devise some criteria for whether a state could possibly become a coalition partner, judging from some objective indicators of its relationship to the proposing state. For instance, we can readily identify all states that are either geographically contiguous to the location of the crisis or are major powers (contiguity on land or within thirteen

6. See, for instance, Gordon and Shapiro 2004.

to twenty-four miles of water).[7] The resulting classification system allows us to build a dataset consisting of a crisis actor and a potential coalition partner. We are then able to examine whether a potential coalition partner became involved on the side of the crisis actor. The analysis also includes control variables for formal alliance ties in order to distinguish between the effects of alliance obligations and multilateral activity and whether the two countries are both democracies.[8] This design is a conservative one, in the sense that it is likely to include many states that are not likely coalition partners, making positive findings especially compelling.

Third, a proper test of the preference similarity hypothesis involves some potentially complicated interaction terms as well as some technical adjustments to account for interdependence in the data. The statistical appendix to this chapter contains a fuller discussion of research design issues and full results, while the following paragraphs simply describe the results in substantive terms.

The results of the statistical analysis can be summarized as follows. First, a Security Council decision in support of the crisis actor increases the probability of an intervener joining by about 5 percent. But there is strong evidence that potential joiners base their decisions on the "credibility" of the signal issued by the Security Council, as indicated by the effect of preference similarity between the crisis actor and the Security Council and the decision of the Security Council. While positive decisions exert a strong pull on potential joiners, the effect is much stronger if the decision is issued from an ideologically distant Council. Just as chapter 3 showed that members of the U.S. public are more likely to support their leaders if authorization is received from an "unlikely" source, so too are potential interveners likely to intervene if authorization is received from a biased source.

To provide some substantive interpretation, when Security Council authorization occurs and the crisis actor has a similarity score with the SC of 0.3, a moderately similar score, the probability of intervention drops about 4 percent from the case of a completely neutral score of 0. When the similarity score is −.3, the probability of intervention increases about 2 percent from the case of complete neutrality. Although these changes appear slight, they represent substantial increases over no authorization. The baseline probability

7. Data on contiguity and major power status is from Eugene (Bennett and Stam 2000), available at http://eugenesoftware.org.
8. There is some debate on the factors that make allies more or less reliable (see Lipson 2003; Leeds 2003; Gartzke and Gleditsch 2004). At least one other study has been found that joint democracy exerts little effect on coming to the aid of targets in militarized disputes (Reiter and Stam 2002).

of intervention under no authorization is nearly 50 percent lower when the similarity score is 0.

The joint effect of the crisis actor and the potential joiner's similarity score under no authorization, however, is important. Potential coalition partners are more likely to join under no authorization if either (a) they are both ideologically distant from the Security Council or (b) they are both ideologically similar to the Security Council. In other words, under no authorization, similarity between the intervener and the crisis actor improves the chances that the intervener will join.

Generally speaking, these results are consistent with those in previous chapters in that they suggest that the effect of organizational decisions depends on how an organization's interests are perceived. The dynamic becomes slightly more complicated by affinity between a potential intervener and a state undertaking a foreign policy initiative, but controlling for that affinity the ideological distance between the intervener and the UN seems to moderate the coalition-building abilities of that UN in the way predicted by the informational theory. In other words, while IOs may help facilitate cooperation, their ability to do so may be contingent on their ability to credibly signal information to foreign audiences, loosening domestic constraints, and allowing governments to cooperate.

CONCLUSION

This chapter examined whether states are more likely to support other countries that receive authorization from (potentially) biased multilateral bodies, weighing in on debates about the international face of legitimacy by examining whether and how IO decisions influence foreign audiences and foreign governments. In this way, it provides support for the ideas of scholars, like Alexander Thompson (2006, 2009), who suggest that security institutions can help states initiating foreign policies signal benign intent to foreign audiences. In turn, this can alleviate domestic constraints among potential allies, facilitating coalition building. The determinants of international legitimacy have important implications for the ability of institutions to alter states' foreign policy behavior, as states often attempt to garner multilateral authorization in order to gain allies or improve their chances of foreign policy success.

The informational logic developed in previous chapters and extended here makes several novel claims about the ability of IOs to facilitate coalition building. In particular, potential allies should be more likely to join a crisis actor that receives multilateral support, particularly if that support comes from an unlikely source. Allies may also be more likely to join crisis actors with similar foreign policy preferences. Finally, allies should act in accordance with institutional decisions more often when those decisions come from multilateral bodies that share their foreign policy preferences.

These conditional claims explain why there is considerable cross-national variation in attitudes toward international organizations, as well as considerable variation in attitudes toward different institutions. The theory also helps explain why governments spend energy lobbying for IO support and frequently advertise IO support globally in efforts to assuage citizens' fears and gain material and political support for their foreign policies.

Some supplementary statistical analysis examined whether preference similarity and organizational decisions affect the decisions of states to join crisis actors. The results support the claims that multilateral authorization, and in particular authorization from a biased Security Council, make allied participation more likely. These results are also consistent with findings from the previous chapters that show that the U.S. public is more likely to rally in response to international disputes when a conservative Security Council issues a supportive ruling and that states, in general, are more likely to consult the Security Council as it becomes more conservative. These results, together with the analysis in chapter 4, demonstrate that the dual faces of political legitimacy for foreign policy—domestic and international—operate according to similar dynamics. Authorization from a biased source appears to foster more legitimacy than that from a neutral or friendly source. The informational argument provides a powerful explanation for these phenomena.

APPENDIX: STATISTICAL EVIDENCE

The informational theory predicts that both the crisis actor's similarity to the Security Council and that of the potential joiner, as well as their similarity to one another, determine the joiner's propensity to join with the conflict. First, the crisis actor's similarity to the Security Council indicates the credibility of the signal. When that similarity is large, authorization should be a strong influence for other states to join with the crisis actor. However, when that similarity is small, authorization may be discounted. The reverse is true for failure to obtain authorization or no authorization. When the similarity between the crisis actor and the Security Council is small, failure to obtain authorization is likely to discourage potential allies, while when the similarity is large failure to obtain authorization is likely to be discounted by potential allies.

Second, the similarity between the potential joiner and the Security Council indicates whether the observer (the audience in the potential joiner state) views its preferences as aligned with the signaler (the Security Council). When that similarity is small, joiners should be more likely to join the crisis actor given a signal of authorization. When that similarity is large, authorization is likely to have little effect, but opposition will also not likely discourage potential allies.

Third, similarity between the potential ally and the crisis actor may have an effect on behavior. Regardless of Security Council activity, potential interveners should be more likely to join states with similar foreign policy preferences.

One might also expect the three factors—authorization, crisis actor–Security Council similarity, and potential joiner–Security Council similarity—to have an interactive effect. I interact these three variables as well as their constituent variables in order to test these hypotheses (see Brambor, Clark, and Golder 2006). In table 5A.1 I list these components, interactions, interpretation, and expected sign, where A is the crisis actor and I is the potential intervener.

Note that the effects of final two terms, the interaction between A's and I's respective similarity scores with the Security Council and the triple interaction term, are indeterminate. This is because the similarity between the crisis actor and the Security Council and that between the potential intervener and the Security Council have countervailing expectations for the intervener's decision. Whereas joiners are most likely to join when the crisis actor receives authorization from a Security Council that is ideologically distant from the crisis actor, joiners are less likely to join when authorization

TABLE 5A.1   Interaction terms and interpretation

TERM	INTERPRETATION	EXPECTED SIGN
SC decision in favor of A	Decision in favor of A when both similarity scores to SC = 0, completely neutral	Moderate positive effect
A's similarity to SC	A's similarity with no authorization and I's similarity to SC = 0	Moderate negative effect or no effect
I's similarity to SC	I's similarity with no authorization and A's similarity to SC = 0	Moderate negative effect or no effect
A's similarity*SC decision in favor of A	A's similarity score with authorization and I's similarity to SC = 0	Negative effect
I's similarity*SC decision in favor of A	I's similarity score with authorization and A's similarity to SC = 0	Positive effect
I's similarity*A's similarity	The joint effect of I's similarity with the SC and A's similarity with the SC with no authorization	Negative effect if both are positive; Positive effect if both are negative; otherwise indeterminate effect
A's similarity*I's similarity*SC decision in favor of I	The joint effect of both I and A similarity to SC with authorization	Strongly positive effect if I's similarity is positive and A's similarity is negative; otherwise weakly positive or indeterminate effect

Note: A, the crisis actor; I, potential intervener.

is observed from a Security Council that is ideologically distant from the intervener.

I include two additional controls: joint democracy and whether the crisis actor and the potential joiner were parties to a defense pact. The coding for defense pacts are from the Correlates of War alliance data, as incorporated in Eugene. Although there is some debate on the factors that make allies more or less reliable (see Leeds 2003; Gartzke and Gleditsch 2004), a defense pact indicates some prior commitment to come to the aid of another signatory. Joint democracy is operationalized as a dummy variable coded as 1 if both the crisis actor and the potential joiner have Polity IV democracy scores of 7 or higher and 0 otherwise. Although joint democracy has been found to exert little effect on coming to the aid of targets in militarized disputes (Reiter and Stam 2002), I control for the possibility that regime type affects the decision of joiners during crises. Finally, I control for whether the crisis was an intra-war crisis, the gravity of the dispute, and for the power status of the crisis actor.

TABLE 5A.2   Probit regression of decision to join in crises

VARIABLE	COEFFICIENT (STANDARD ERROR)
SC decision in favor of A	2.546* (1.018)
A's similarity to SC	−1.248** (.352)
I's similarity to SC	−.144 (.283)
A's similarity*SC decision in favor of A	−2.178* (.953)
I's similarity*SC decision in favor of A	−.921 (2.421)
I's similarity to SC*A's similarity to SC	.887* (.385)
A's similarity*I's similarity*SC decision in favor of I	.314 (2.418)
Defense pact	−.285* (.139)
Joint democracy	−.217 (.198)
Intrawar crisis	−.007 (.031)
Power status of crisis actor	.186* (.092)
Gravity	−.032 (.051)
Constant	1.509** (.174)
N	715
χ^2	34.95**
Log Pseudolikelihood	−244.113

Note: A, the crisis actor; I, potential intervener.
*Significant at the .05 level. 166 clusters.
**Significant at the .01 level.

Due to the dichotomous dependent variable I employ a probit estimator. The data are structured such that although each observation is a unique pair of a crisis actor and "politically relevant" intervener, there may be more than one observation for crisis if a crisis has multiple actors. I therefore compute standard errors clustered by crisis to account for nonindependence across crises.

After accounting for missing data on similarity scores, the sample is reduced to an n of 715 encompassing 166 distinct crises from 1946 to 2002. The coefficients and standard errors are displayed in table 5A.2.

The following results shed light on the coalition-building effect of Security Council activity. First, a Security Council decision in support of the crisis actor increases the probability of an intervener joining by about 5 percent. While positive decisions exert a strong pull on potential joiners, the effect is much stronger if the decision is issued from an ideologically distant

Council. This is demonstrated by the coefficient on a positive decision times the crisis actor's similarity to the Security Council.

The triple interaction, which is the most likely term to have an indeterminate effect, is statistically insignificant. The joint effect of the crisis actor and the potential joiner's similarity score under no authorization, however, is positive, which suggests that potential joiners s are more likely to join under no authorization if either (a) they are both ideologically distant from the Security Council or (b) they are both ideologically similar to the Security Council. In other words, under no authorization, similarity between the intervener and the crisis actor improves the chances that the intervener will join. When one score is negative and the other score positive, as would be the case if the crisis actor was similar to the Security Council and the potential joiner distant, the net effect decreases the probability of joining.

There is little evidence that potential joiners base their decisions on their own distance to the Security Council, however. On the one hand, the theory predicts that the potential intervener's similarity to the Security Council should have little effect when the Security Council does not issue a ruling. This claim is supported in the data. On the other hand, the interaction between a positive ruling in favor of the crisis actor and the potential intervener's similarity to the Security Council should exert a positive effect. As the intervener has more in common with the signaler or agent (the Security Council), authorization should boost the chances of joining. Instead, the results suggest that interveners pay more attention to the preference relationship between the Security Council and the appealing actor.

APPENDIX: FORMAL THEORETICAL DISCUSSION

Begin by considering the foreign audience's belief updating upon seeing the behavior of the proposing state and the multilateral institution. The proposing state should only propose policies that it prefers to the status quo. First, it is weakly dominant to propose a policy multilaterally if the pivotal member will support, as the proposing state can at most be indifferent between unilateral andt multilateral proposals in such an instance. However, the proposer may also be indifferent regarding multilateral and unilateral proposals if she expects institutional opposition. Thus, all the foreign audience can conclude from a multilateral or unilateral proposal is that the $x \leq 2x_p$, or that the proposer prefers x to the status quo.

For a unilateral offer, this means that the foreign audience must issue its support knowing only that $0 < x \leq 2x_p$. Integrating over this range and comparing expected utility,

$$\int_0^{2x_p} -(0 - x_{FA})^2 U dx \leq \int_0^{2x_p} -(x - x_{FA})^2 U dx$$

The foreign audience will support the policy if $x_{FA} \geq \dfrac{x_p}{3}$. The foreign audience cannot be too conservative compared to the proposing state in order to support unilateral action. We assumed previously, however, that the foreign audience only knows x_p with some error. Let $e \sim \theta(\mu, \sigma)$ represent the error surround the foreign audience's estimate of the proposing state's ideal point. If $x_{FA} \geq \dfrac{E[x_p]}{3}$, the audience will continue to support the policy.

Let γ be the cost to the potential intervening state of acting against the opinion the foreign audience. Without the implementation stage, assume that the actors indicate their pure policy preferences. Note that this is equivalent to assuming that the policy is only implemented if the intervening state chooses to join. Relaxing this assumption would allow for a range of conditions under which the potential intervener could not affect the policy outcome, a situation in which the intervener would be simply indifferent.

We know that given that a policy proposal has been made and that the foreign audience indicates its support, the intervening state faces the following calculation:

$$-(0 - x_I)^2 \leq -(x - x_I)^2$$

and supports if $x \leq 2x_I$.

The multilateral case allows the foreign audience to observe both the proposing state and the decision of the IO. The degree of updating again depends on the position of the pivotal IO member's ideal point relative to the proposing state and the foreign audience. If the IO member's ideal point is to the left of the foreign audience, the audience will update its beliefs with certainty that the policy is within its range of preferable policies and will indicate its support. This, again, is conditional on the nature of error surrounding the foreign audience's perception of the pivotal member's ideal point.

If the pivotal member's ideal point is between the foreign audience's and the proposing state's ideal points, the foreign audience again faces an unexpected utility calculation of the form:

$$\int_0^{2x_M} -(0-x_{FA})^2 U dx \leq \int_0^{2x_M} -(x-x_{FA})^2 U dx$$

Solving reveals that the audience will support if $x_{FA} \geq \dfrac{E[x_M]}{3}$. This threshold is again easier to meet as x_M decreases, or as the pivotal member becomes more conservative or closer in preference relationship to the foreign audience.

There is also a class of babbling equilibria in which the institution sometimes opposes and sometimes supports the appealing state and the signal is not conditional on whether the appealing state has, in fact, suggested a reasonable policy initiative. This possibility would again introduce "noise" into foreign audience's expectations. However, as in chapter 2, I appeal to the notion that states on the Security Council have an incentive to try to signal their preferences, as it is costless and can only help sway the eventual outcome in their favor. We could thus impose an off-equilibrium path belief that the audience updates its beliefs as if the signal is sincere in the off-equilibrium path instance that the pivotal member sends a signal other than its sincere interests, which would make the public more likely to support the policy that the pivotal member opposes.

CONCLUSION

Why have the United Nations and other regional security organizations flourished in the second half of the twentieth century? Aside from the major power Concert of Europe and the short-lived League of Nations, the post-1945 world in which the UN Security Council and a number of a regional organizations have developed and thrived is peculiar when pitted against the entire post-Westphalia international system. Multilateral security IOs continue to play a central role in world affairs. As of this writing, the Obama administration is working actively through the United Nations on new initiatives to combat nuclear proliferation and the political life of the UN appears alive and well, despite dire post–Iraq War predictions that the institution would fade into irrelevance. Why do these institutions exist and what effect do they have on international affairs? Why would states ever ask for approval when conducting policies that determine their own security? Why is it ever in states' interests to defer to a body of other states that may very well be collectively biased against their interests?

This book provides several new answers to these questions. The central argument of the book is that multilateral security institutions provide an important third-party source of information in world affairs. This is particularly important for democratic audiences, who have at their disposal means of holding their leaders accountable for overly aggressive foreign policies, but these bodies may also serve valuable functions for any political actor wanting to acquire more information about potential foreign policy outcomes. In turn, the fact that leaders may depend on these institutions to get support, both at home and abroad, for policies that are potentially controversial and may engender costly political opposition, means that the presence of these institutions can alter political incentives in important ways. To the extent that these institutions can provide "political cover," it is strategically beneficial to seek out their approval, which means that leaders may moderate their foreign policies in order to garner approval or avoid proposals that will provoke widespread international opposition.[1]

Importantly, these answers do not rest on an appeal to norms about deference to international authorities or international legal rules, which vary considerably around the world, or on assumptions about the enforcement mechanisms of international organizations, which are largely absent for the type of institution studied here, but rather on the political incentives these institutions create for governments. In other words, this book goes beyond debates about whether norms or material enforcement matter to analyze more indirect channels of influence that, while focusing on the intangible subject of public statements, providing a rationalist underpinning for institutional influence.

This book therefore provides an answer to the question of how multilateral security institutions can influence politics through cheap talk, but it opens the door for several promising areas of research as well. First, the argument presented throughout the book provides a potentially new lens through which to view institutional design. The informational argument holds that the ability of institutions to convey relevant information depends on two interrelated, alterable features of design: membership and voting rules. Second, the informational logic can potentially be applied to other types of institutions, like the International Monetary Fund (IMF) or WTO, that are frequent subjects of institutional analysis. In many cases, scholars have pointed out indirect ways in which these institutions matter, but how their mandates and decisions are interpreted by third parties, like international markets, has not been a central focus of the relevant literature. The remainder of this concluding chapter will discuss these areas and provide some conjectures for further study.

---

1. Chapman and Wolford (2010) point out, however, that under some conditions favorable IO rulings may facilitate more, not less aggressive demands.

INSTITUTIONAL DESIGN AND EFFECTIVENESS

One promising avenue of recent research revolves around questions of institutional design (e.g., Koremenos, Lipson, and Snidal 2001; Koremenos 2005; Haftel 2007; Morelli and Maggi 2006; Rosendorff 2005; Rosendorff and Milner 2001). This work investigates the optimal design of international institutions and agreements, given some normative or policy goal. It is not immediately clear, however, what the normative goal should be in the context of multilateral security institutions. From a purely pacific viewpoint, and in keeping with the tradition enshrined in the UN charter, one goal might be to maintain international peace and stability by prohibiting the use of force. However, many would argue that the use of force is often necessary to maintain international peace and security, particular in deterring and responding to aggression. If this is the case, the goal of design should be to create an institution that is best equipped to decide upon and monitor *appropriate* uses of force, as defined by some agreed-upon first principles about self-defense and the collective good.

This is, in fact, what the UN charter attempts to achieve (Goodrich 1947; Claude 1969). However, the political realities of the post-1945 world created a conundrum: powerful states demanded a seat at the table, but the goals of the world's most powerful states do not always coincide with the maintenance of international peace and security and the "appropriate" use of force. In fact, this problem was one of the central factors that undermined the League of Nations, as several of the permanent members of the League Council—Italy, Japan, and Germany (until its withdrawal in 1933)—were the most aggressive revisionist states during the interwar period.

Even though the international distribution of power has shifted since the end of World War II with rising developing country powers and the decline of the Soviet Union, this fundamental problem of design remains. The ultimate decision makers within the UN Security Council often have distributive disagreements over outcomes; in other words, the permanent members are unlikely to always have the world collective good in mind when making decisions. Moreover, the states that are most capable of committing aggression in the international system, and with the most global interests that might give rise to disputes, are precisely those tasked with limiting such aggression.

A related question is whether these members could even arrive at a common understanding of the collective good, given the nature of the international system. Yet, this problem is not unlike many other problem of social design, and many philosophers and scholars have put forth answers to how to design institutions to best manage "factions," to adopt from James Madison's phrase in *Federalist No. 10*, that have competing distributive priorities. The central difference when considering international institutions is the lack of an authoritative social and political actor to implement and enforce an agreement or mechanism to deal with competing factions. Agreements must, then, be self-enforcing, in the sense that the actors that are essential for the organization to function must "buy in," or prefer the continued function of the institution to an alternative path that could involve isolation, coercion, or another type of institution altogether (cf. Ikenberry 2001).

How can this be done in the context of a global organization like the UN? Institutions can only be self-enforcing when no party prefers to deviate to some alternative agreement, but this requires that parties can credibly threaten to punish one another or dissolve the institution in the event of a defection.[2] In other words, states must be able to hold each other accountable for decisions that violate some agreement about the greater good. But this again requires some common understanding of the greater good, which is difficult, if not impossible, to arrive at when dealing with distributive issues.

Setting aside the issue of whether sovereign countries could ever agree on the global "good" or credibly threaten to punish one another for military transgressions, we might ask instead how multilateral organizations might be best organized to constrain or moderate aggression and influence foreign policymaking toward actions that are likely to produce peaceful settlements to major disputes. As a starting point to this book, I noted that organizations like the UN are frequently criticized for lacking direct enforcement capabilities. Mandates are enforced only when one of the great powers takes it upon themselves to do so. This suggests that any institution that is premised on policing its members through explicit or implicit punishments for defection must, at a minimum, feature countries that are capable of enforcing its mandates in a prominent and central role, again raising the question "who polices the police?"

This book points to another way in which institutions may influence or moderate aggression—through the channel of public opinion. In this regard, the preferences of key member states have important consequences for the ability of institutions to influence foreign policy behavior. The very preferences that prevent the organization from being able to commonly define the

---

2. On self-enforcing equilibria in other political contexts, see Grief 1998; Milgrom, North, and Weingast 1990; Weingast 1997.

greater good can play a role in generating institutional influence through providing information. The UNSC, as a heterogeneous body with multiple vetoing members, can be influential in legitimizing action precisely because of the likelihood that at least one vetoing member will oppose action, or because the key members often disagree. The institutional features of preference heterogeneity and the veto rule make authorization a very powerful signal that policies will have limited disruptive effects to international order.

At the same time, however, the very features that make the UNSC effective at conveying the limited effects of policies with its support makes it more likely that opposition of one of its permanent members, and thus the absence of institutional support, is discounted by key audiences. In other words, given the difficulty of obtaining consensus among the P-5, failure to do so may be discounted as uninformative, and thus not invoke a public opinion backlash. The ability of member states to credibly threaten to implement opposition can lessen the tendency of audiences to discount opposition, but given the costliness of imposing punishment through sanctions or military action, establishing a credible threat of punishment is often difficult.

The central point, however, is that the political need for approval creates incentives toward moderation, since it requires obtaining consensus. The high "legislative hurdle" of the organization can have the effect of forcing greater moderation in aggressive demands, provided that a leader desires domestic and international public support for his or her policies. Leaders who enjoy *ex ante* high approval ratings and that have the independent ability to acquire allies may eschew the channels of IO approval, as the United States has often done.

It is worth considering whether there may be a trade-off between designing an institution capable of providing legitimacy through authorization, and thus providing incentives for states to seek compromise in order to obtain authorization, and one whose threatened *disapproval* deters states from proposing aggressive foreign policies. Although conservative institutions, such as the UNSC, may be "uniquely positioned" (Malone 2004, 639) to confer legitimacy on foreign policy actions, they may be less effective at constraining expansive policies when compared to institutions like NATO, which is often perceived as dominated by the United States (Malone and Khong 2003). This is because opposition from NATO, from the perspective of the informational theory presented here, is likely to be politically costly and therefore something leaders will avoid. In fact, the perception of U.S. domination of NATO may actually be due to the incentives of U.S. leaders to avoid proposing policies that will receive opposition from NATO. Future work should devote more attention to this balance, as the reform of security institutions, such as the UNSC, must wrestle with this trade-off.[3]

Would altering the current membership or voting rules improve the ability of the UN Security Council to convey information or confer legitimacy on actions? One answer to this question begins with the recognition that the above trade-off is consistent with the conclusions of work on the "informational efficiency" of legislative committee rules (Gilligan and Krehbiel 1988, 462–63; Thompson 2006).[4] Heterogeneity of preferences amongst committee members and nonmajoritarian voting increases informational efficiency because policy approval signals that even the most conservative members of a body (in a veto or consensus context) approve of the policy. Signals of *opposition*, however, are common with preference heterogeneity and nonmajoritarian voting rules. Opposition signals only that *at least* one vetoing member disagrees with the policy, and thus may occur in a wide variety of circumstances. In such circumstances, institutional decisions may be noisy or convey little about underlying policy merit.

Moving to majoritarian voting in the Security Council would have the effect of reducing the voting power of preference outliers while shifting influence to a "pivot" state. Relative to the veto system, which preserves the power of the most extreme preference outliers among the P-5, a majority rule would shift the pivotal member closer to the median world member. This lowers the "legislative hurdle" of the institution, meaning that passing resolutions would become easier. In turn, the institution would authorize more policies, which could actually *reduce* its influence, particularly if greater rates of authorization mean that the institution authorizes a wider range of possible policies. In the language of the theory in this book, from the naive observer's viewpoint, authorizing a wider range of possible foreign policy initiatives would reduce the ability to update one's beliefs about the likely outcome of policies in the aftermath of seeing authorization. Assuming that the same states remain permanent members, moving to majority rule would, in essence, shift the legislative hurdle to in between an institution that is extremely "conservative" and one that is extremely "revisionist"

3. On the future of UN legitimacy in wake of the 2003 Iraq War, see Glennon 2003; Tharoor 2003; Malone 2004; and Marfleet and Miller 2005.
4. Rogers also demonstrates the incentives for legislators "to create and maintain independent, policy-motivated judiciaries" (2001, 85). Allowing judiciary review on the basis of independent preferences is also more informationally efficient.

or "permissive." Therefore, it is far from clear that moving to a more majoritarian form of voting would improve institutional effectiveness.

Another type of reform proposal involves adding more veto players. The informational effect of expanding permanent membership of the Security Council and granting states such as Brazil or India seats is indeterminate, as heterogeneity would increase but the current P-5 would likely continue to be seen as preference outliers in many circumstances. Of course, if the veto were maintained under such an expansion, relative voting power would be redistributed (O'Neill 1996). If the new permanent members were granted a veto, it could increase the legitimacy effect of an authorization signal, because it would signal consensus amongst a wider group of states. The downside of such a reform would be that it may become prohibitively difficult to pass any resolution that is more than a purely symbolic statement. However, if a shift to majority rule were to accompany expanded membership, the situation would again be one of shifting the "pivot," likely lowering the legislative hurdle.

Normative perspectives start from different first principals to identify some other factors that might affect the legitimacy of IOs. From the point of view of the theory and evidence presented here, we might think of these normative factors as institutional characteristics that influence how closely people pay attention to an information source in the first place. That is, while information provision might remain unchanged by simply adding more members, undertaking reforms that that make an institution seem more "fair" to observers might increase its visibility, or the frequency with which people pay attention to its decisions. Scholars have suggested that institutions are more likely to be perceived as legitimate if they are "depoliticized" or more inclusive in membership and decision making (Barnett and Finnemore 1999, 412; Grant and Keohane 2005, 35). In this way current reform proposals that recommend increasing membership of the UN Security may be worthwhile undertakings. Shifting to a majority voting rule, however, would likely reduce institutional influence, while expanding the veto might increase institutional influence at the cost of making agreement, and thus passing any meaningful resolution, quite rare.

APPLICATIONS TO OTHER INSTITUTIONS

A separate line of research might ask whether the informational logic applies to other types of institutions, such as the WTO or IMF? To the extent that decisions are influential in the way that they reflect perceived biases of these institutions, the logic identified here can be applied to many other types of organizations, even outside the realm of security affairs. There are three key factors to keep in mind with respect to applying the logic of public reaction to the decisions of other organizations, and how this reaction interacts with foreign policy.

The first factor is the means of enforcement that an institution has at its disposal. The IMF, for instance, may suspend loans to countries in the face of noncompliance, although political incentives of major donors may frequently undermine the credibility of this enforcement mechanism (Stone 2004). The WTO lacks independent enforcement power; instead it ability to influence states lies in its adjudication procedures and rulings, which can authorize retaliation for trade sanctions (Reinhardt 2001). In this way, the pure informational logic may be more applicable to institutions like the WTO, which rely on member states to enact punishment. For instance, countries shouldering the burden of enforcement may view WTO rulings as useful for convincing domestic factions that are possibly hurt by trade competition that a particular enforcement action or trade retaliation is warranted, thus alleviating the political costs of retaliation.[5]

The idea that economic institutions may also provide key information to important political actors points to another key factor in institutional effectiveness: the identity of decision makers within an institution. The WTO dispute settlement mechanism relies on a panel of professional, objective international trade law experts. In this way it is close to an "altruistic" institution, as its interests lie only in ruling against clear violations and authorizing appropriate retaliation.[6] The IMF governing structure is closer to the UN Security Council, in that IMF decisions are driven by the preferences of large donors due to its quota based voting system (Oatley and Yackee 2004; Stone 2004). There is, in fact, evidence that the credibility of IMF enforcement is undermined by this institutional feature (Stone 2004). In other words, the relevant bias of the institution influences outcomes, undermining the ability of the institution to influence compliance with reforms aimed at alleviating problems of chronic fiscal insolvency. This bias is a direct function of the states or actors that determine decisions within the organization—a feature of design that can be negotiated and revised.

The third factor to consider is the extent to which an organization's decisions are visible and whether relevant target audiences are capable of in-

---

5. Vreeland (2003) makes a related point about governments "scapegoating" the IMF in order to make liberal reforms in the face of domestic opposition.
6. To the extent that its rulings are "principled" or based on some consistent legal rules, it more resembles an institution that is legitimate, as pointed out by Voeten (2005).

fluencing their government and leaders. That is, if organizations can exert influence by providing information to key constituencies, we must consider whether organizational activity is public, whether the constituencies that matter care, and whether those constituencies have at their disposal the ability to influence elected officials controlling foreign policy. Throughout this book the focus has been primarily on domestic audiences. Foreign audiences may also matter for incentivizing leaders to seek external authorization for military policies. The decisions of the WTO, on the other hand, affect consumers and producers at home and abroad, although the most likely audience to devote close attention to the technical process of dispute settlement is the group of domestic producers affected by an alleged unfair trade practice. There is evidence that third parties actually devote considerable attention to the WTO dispute settlement process (Busch and Reinhardt 2006). IMF programs affect an even more diffuse group of political actors through various austerity measures, and anti-liberalization domestic interests likely view IMF decisions with intense interest (Vreeland 2003). The central point is that the relevant constituencies, as well as the degree to which decisions are public and the details of decisions are accessible, may differ across institutional contexts. Therefore, when looking for evidence of indirect influence through information channels one must keep in mind how relevant features of institutions affect the process.

The core theoretical points that may be relevant for "transporting" the informational theory to other institutional contexts are that institutional design can influence outside perceptions of IOs and thus the credibility of their signals and that this may affect third-party actors in ways that create interesting political incentives for governments forming foreign military or economic policy. Although considerable attention has been paid to domestic-international linkages in recent years, the informational channel of influence has received less attention.[7]

FUTURE DIRECTIONS

This book argued that multilateral security institutions matter because they influence domestic politics by providing relevant information to critical audiences. In turn, leaders often seek external approval for political benefits. Even though these leaders may be interested first and foremost with national security and realist considerations, the need for proximate political

7. For work that touches on these themes, see Milner 1997; Mansfield, Milner, and Rosendorff 2002; Mansfield and Pevehouse 2005.

survival creates incentives to seek the approval of "toothless" organizations. This incentive exists even when there is no legal obligation for consultation or legal punishment for circumventing institutional channels.

The logic underlying this claim provided several unique and testable hypotheses about when leaders consult international institutions and how institutional decisions effect domestic and international outcomes. Large-n, experimental, and anecdotal qualitative evidence provide support for these hypotheses. Taken together, the empirical chapters of this book identify several patterns supporting of the informational argument.

This conclusion has indentified two issues that deserve more scholarly attention, however. The first is the optimal design of multilateral security institutions. This question is complex for the reasons identified above as well as for the political realities that are involved with negotiating design and reform. Powerful states will continue to want a privileged position, while less powerful states will want guarantees of restraint. Identifying optimal design also requires that scholars take inspiration from multiple theoretical traditions, as the rationalist perspective presented in this book is relatively silent on what people in developing countries will find "fair" in a normative sense. Yet clearly the degree to which representation is descriptive and/or substantive is a factor that influences how people regard institutions.

The second issue is the degree to which this logic is generalizable across institutional context. Understanding whether the preferences of institutions like the WTO or IMF influence or partially determine institutional effectiveness is critical for understanding the optimal design of those institutions, as well. While some significant progress has been made in this direction (e.g., Stone 2004; Oatley and Yackee 2004), it is worth considering the possible directions for reform and the political possibilities of reform of these other important institutions.

Although these questions remain unresolved, the arguments developed in this book point toward a novel avenue for understanding how institutions matter in world affairs. As a broader point, however, this book illustrates the need for divergent theoretical perspectives to identify their common assumptions and the observable implications that flow from those assumptions in order to make sense of the empirical world. These methodological points are not mere esoteric scholarly concerns; rather, they determine how we think about designing better and more effective institutions. Without careful analysis of this sort, we cannot say anything meaningful about our ultimate normative questions of concern—namely, what are the best ways to organize institutions and agreements to make the world a more peaceful place.

REFERENCES

Abbott, Kenneth W., Robert Keohane, Andrew Moravcisk, Anne-Marie Slaughter, and Duncan Snidal. 2000. "The Concept of Legalization." *International Organization* 54 (3): 401–19.

Abbott, Kenneth W., and Duncan Snidal. 1998. "Why States Act through Formal International Organizations." *Journal of Conflict Resolution* 42 (1): 3–32.

Aldrich, John H., Christopher Gelpi, Peter Feaver, Jason Reifler, and Kristin Thompson Sharp. 2006. "Foreign Policy and the Electoral Connection." *Annual Review of Political Science* 120 (1): 35–57.

Aldrich, John H., John L. Sullivan, and Eugene Borgida. 1989. "Foreign Affairs and Issue Voting: Do Presidential Candidates 'Waltz Before a Blind Audience?'" *American Political Science Review* 83: 123–41.

Almond, Gabriel. 1950. *The American People and Foreign Policy.* New York: Harcourt, Brace.

Amemiya, Takeshi. 1973. "Regression Analysis when the Dependent Variable Is Truncated Normal." *Econometrica* 41 (6): 997–1016.

Arend, Anthony Clark, and Robert J. Beck. 1993. *International Law and the Use of Force: Beyond the UN Charter Paradigm.* New York: Routledge.

Austen-Smith, David, and Jeffrey S. Banks. 2000. "Cheap Talk and Burned Money." *Journal of Economic Theory* 91 (1): 1–16.

Baker, William D., and John R. Oneal. 2001. "Patriotism or Opinion Leadership: The Nature and Origins of the 'Rally' Round the Flag' Effect." *Journal of Conflict Resolution* 45 (5): 661–87.

Barnett, Michael 1997. "Bringing in the New World Order: Legitimacy, Liberalism, and the United Nations." *World Politics* 49 (4): 526–51.

Barnett, Michael, and Martha Finnemore. 1999. "The Politics, Power, and Pathologies of International Organizations." *International Organization* 53 (4): 699–732.

Baum, Matthew. 2002. "The Constituent Foundations of the Rally-Round-the-Flag Phenomena." *International Studies Quarterly* 46: 263–98.

————. 2003. *Soft News Goes to War: Public Opinion and American Foreign Policy in the New Media Age.* Princeton, NJ: Princeton University Press.

————. 2004. "Going Private: Public Opinion, Presidential Rhetoric, and the *Domestic* Politics of Audience Costs in U.S. Foreign Policy Crises." *Journal of Conflict Resolution* 48(5): 603–631.

Baum, Matthew, and David Lake. 2003. "The Political Economy of Growth: Democracy and Human Capital." *American Journal of Political Science* 43: 333–47.

Baum, Matthew, and Phillip Potter. 2008. "The Relationship between Mass Media, Public Opinion and Foreign Policy: Toward a Theoretical Synthesis." *Annual Review of Political Science* 11: 39–66.

Bawn, Kathleen. 1995. "Political Control versus Expertise: Congressional Choices about Administrative Procedures." *American Political Science Review* 89 (1): 61–73.

Beck, Robert J. 1993. *The Grenada Invasion: Politics, Law, and Foreign Policy Decisionmaking.* Boulder, CO: Westview Press.

Bennett, D. Scott, and Allan Stam. 2000. "*EUGene:* A Conceptual Manual." *International Interactions* 26: 179–204.

Boehmer, Charles, Erik Gartzke, and Timothy Nordstrom. 2004. "Do Intergovernmental Organizations Promote Peace?" *World Politics* 57(1): 1–38.

Brambor, Thomas, William Roberts Clark, and Matt Golder. 2006. "Understanding Interaction Models: Improving Empirical Analyses." *Political Analysis* 14: 63–82.

Braumoeller, Bear. 2004. "Hypothesis Testing and Multiplicative Interaction Terms." *International Organization* 58: 807–20.

Brecher, Michael, and Jonathan Wilkenfeld. 2000. *A Study of Crisis.* Ann Arbor: University of Michigan Press.

————. 2006. *International Crisis Behavior Project Codebook.* http://www.cidcm.umd.edu/icb/data.

Brecher, Michael, Jonathan Wilkenfeld, and Sheila Moser. 1988. *Crises in the Twentieth Century: Handbook of International Crises.* Vol. 1. New York: Pergamon.

Brody, Richard. 1991. *Assessing the President.* Palo Alto, CA: Stanford University Press.

Brooks, Stephen G., and William C. Wohlforth. 2005. "International Relations Theory and the Case against Unilateralism." *Perspective on Politics* 3 (3): 509–24.

Brownlee, Jason. 2007. *Authoritarianism in an Age of Democratization.* New York: Cambridge University Press.

Bueno de Mesquita, Bruce, Alastair Smith, Randolph Siverson, and James D. Morrow. 1999. "An Institutional Explanation of the Democratic Peace." *American Political Science Review* 93 (4): 791–807.

———. 2003. *The Logic of Political Survival.* Cambridge, MA: MIT Press.

Busch, Marc. 2007. "Overlapping Institutions, Forum Shopping, and Dispute Settlement in International Trade." *International Organization* 61 (4): 735–61.

Busch, Marc, and Eric Reinhardt. 2006. "Three's a Crowd: Third Parties and WTO Dispute Settlement." *World Politics* 58: 446–77.

Bush, George H. W., and Brent Scowcroft. 1998. *A World Transformed.* New York: Vintage Books.

Calvert, Randall. 1985. "The Value of Biased Information: A Rational Choice Model of Political Advice." *Journal of Politics* 47: 530–55.

Campbell, Angus, Philip E. Converse, Warren E. Miller, and Donald E. Stokes. 1964. *The American Voter.* New York: John Wiley.

Carr, E. H. 1939. *The Twenty Years' Crisis, 1919–1939.* New York: Harper and Row.

Carrubba, Clifford J. 2009. "A Model of the Endogenous Development of Judicial Institutions in Federal and International Systems." *Journal of Politics* 71 (1): 55–69.

Carrubba, Clifford J., Amy Yuen, and Christopher Zorn. 2007. "In Defense of Comparative Statics: Specifying Empirical Tests of Models of Strategic Interaction." *Political Analysis* 15 (4): 465–82.

Chapman, Terrence. 2007. "International Security Institutions, Domestic Politics, and Institutional Legitimacy." *Journal of Conflict Resolution* 51 (1): 134–66.

———. 2009. "Audience Beliefs and International Organization Legitimacy." *International Organization* 63 (4): 733–64.

Chapman, Terrence, and Dan Reiter. 2004. "The United Nations Security Council and the Rally 'Round the Flag Effect." *Journal of Conflict Resolution* 48 (6): 886–909.

Chapman, Terrence, and Scott Wolford. 2010. "International Organizations, Strategy, and Crisis Bargaining. *Journal of Politics* 72 (1): 227–42.

Chayes, Abram, and Antonia Handler Chayes. 1993. "On Compliance." *International Organization* 47 (2): 175–205.

————. 1995. *The New Sovereignty: Compliance with International Regulatory Agreements.* Cambridge, MA: Harvard University Press.

Claude, Inis L. Jr. 1966. "Collective Legitimization as a Political Function of the United Nations." *International Organization* 20 (3): 367–79.

————. 1969. "The United Nations, the United States, and the Maintenance of International Peace." *International Organization* 23 (3): 621–36.

Colaresi, Michael. 2007. "The Benefit of Doubt: Testing an Informational Theory of the Rally Effect." *International Organization* 61 (1): 93–143.

Coleman, Katharina. 2007. *International Organizations and Peace Enforcement: The Politics of International Legitimacy.* New York: Cambridge University Press.

Cowhey, Peter F. 1990. "The International Telecommunications Regime: The Political Roots of Regimes of High Technology." *International Organization* 44 (2): 169–99.

Crawford, Vincent P., and Joel Sobel. 1982. "Strategic Information Transmission." *Econometrica* 50 (6): 1431–51.

Dai, Xinyuan. 2005. "Why Comply? The Domestic Constituency Mechanism." *International Organization* 59 (2): 363–98.

Danilovic, Vesna. 2001. "Conceptual and Selection Bias Issues in Deterrence." *Journal of Conflict Resolution* 45 (1): 97–125.

Dassell, Kurt, and Eric Reinhardt. 1999. "Domestic Strife and the Initiation of Violence at Home and Abroad." *American Journal of Political Science* 43 (1): 56–85.

Deroun, Karl Jr. 2000. "Presidents and the Diversionary Use of Force: A Research Note." *International Studies Quarterly* 44 (2): 317–28.

Dixon, William. 1993. "Democracy and the Management of International Conflict." *Journal of Conflict Resolution* 37 (1): 42–68.

————. 1994. "Democracy and the Peaceful Settlement of International Conflict." *American Political Science Review* 88 (March): 14–32.

Downs, George W., David M. Rocke, and Peter N. Barsoom. 1996. "Is the Good News about Compliance Good News about Cooperation?" *International Organization* 50 (3): 379–406.

Doyle, Michael. 1986. "Liberalism and World Politics." *American Political Science Review* 80 (4): 1151–61.

Dreher, Axel, Jan-Egbert Sturm, and James Raymond Vreeland. 2009. "Development Aid and International Politics: Does Membership on the

UN Security Council Influence World Bank Decisions?" *Journal of Development Economics* 88: 1–18.

Drezner, Dan. 2000. "Bargaining, Enforcement, and Multilateral Economic Sanctions: When Is Cooperation Counterproductive?" *International Organization* 54 (4): 73–102.

———, ed. 2003. *Locating the Proper Authorities: The Interaction of Domestic and International Institutions.* Ann Arbor: University of Michigan Press.

Edwards, George C. 1980. *Presidential Influence in Congress.* San Francisco, CA: Freeman.

Eichenberg, Richard. 2005. "Victory Has Many Friends: U.S. Public Opinion and the Use of Military Force, 1981–2005." *International Security* 30 (1): 140–77.

Fang, Songying. 2008. "The Informational Role of International Institutions and Domestic Politics." *American Journal of Political Science* 52 (2): 304–21.

Farrell, Joseph. 1995. "Talk Is Cheap." *American Economic Review* 85 (2): 186–90.

Farrell, Joseph, and Robert Gibbons. 1989. "Cheap Talk with Two Audiences." *American Economic Review* 79 (5): 1214–23.

Farrell, Joseph, and Matthew Rabin. 1996. "Cheap Talk." *Journal of Economic Perspectives* 10 (3): 103–18.

Fearon, James D. 1994. "Domestic Political Audiences and the Escalation of International Disputes." *American Political Science Review* 88 (3): 577–92.

———. 1997. "Signaling Foreign Policy Interests: Tying Hands versus Sinking Costs." *Journal of Conflict Resolution* 41: 68–90.

———. 2002. "Selection Effects and Deterrence." *International Interactions* 28 (1): 5–29.

Fearon, James D., and David Laitin. 2004. "Neotrusteeship and the Problem of Weak States." *International Security* 28 (4): 5–43.

Finnemore, Martha. 1996. *National Interests in International Society.* Ithaca, NY: Cornell University Press.

Fiorina, Morris. 1981. *Retrospective Voting in American National Elections.* New Haven, CT: Yale University Press.

Franck, Thomas. 1990. *The Power of Legitimacy among Nations.* New York: Oxford University Press.

Gandhi, Jennifer. 2008. *Political Institutions under Dictatorship.* New York: Cambridge University Press.

Garrett, Geoffrey, and Barry Weingast. 1993. "Ideas, Interests, and Institutions: Constructing the European Community's Internal Market." In *Ideas and Foreign Policy: Beliefs, Institutions, and Political Change*, ed. Judith Goldstein and Robert O. Keohane, 173–206. Ithaca, NY: Cornell University Press.

Gartner, Scott Sigmund. 2008. "The Multiple Effects of Casualties on Public Support for War: An Experimental Approach." *American Political Science Review* 102 (1): 95–106.

Gartner, Scott Sigmund, and Gary Segura. 1998. "War, Casualties, and Public Opinion." *Journal of Conflict Resolution* 42 (3): 278–300.

Gartzke, Erik. 1998. "Kant We All Just Get Along? Opportunity, Willingness, and the Origins of the Democratic Peace." *American Journal of Political Science* 42 (1): 1–27.

Gartzke, Erik, and Kristian Skrede Gledisch. 2004. "Why Democracies May Actually Be Less Reliable Allies." *American Journal of Political Science* 48 (4): 775–95.

Gelpi, Christopher, Peter D. Feaver, and Jason Reifler. 2005–2006. "Success Matters: Casualty Sensitivity and the War in Iraq." *International Security* 30 (3): 7–46.

Gilligan, Thomas W., and Keith Krehbiel. 1988. "Asymmetric Information and Legislative Rules with a Heterogeneous Committee." *American Journal of Political Science* 33 (2): 459–90.

——. 1990. "Organization of Informative Committees by a Rational Legislature." *American Journal of Political Science* 34 (2): 531–64.

Glennon, Michael. 2001. *Limits of Law, Prerogatives of Power: Interventionism after Kosovo.* New York: Palgrave Macmillan.

——. 2003. "Why the Security Council Failed." *Foreign Affairs* 82 (3): 16–35.

Gochman, Charles S., and Zeev Maoz. 1984. "Militarized Interstate Disputes, 1816–1976: Procedures, Patterns and Insights." *Journal of Conflict Resolution* 28: 485–615.

Goldsmith, Jack, and Daryl Levinson. 2008. "Law for States: International Law, Constitutional Law, Public Law." *Harvard International Law Review* 122 (7): 1791–868.

Goldstein, Judith O., Miles Kahler, Robert Keohane, and Anne-Marie Slaughter. 2000. "Introduction: Legalization and World Politics." *International Organization* 54 (3): 385–99.

Goodrich, Leland M. 1947. "From League of Nations to United Nations." *International Organization* 1 (1): 3–21.

——. 1965. "The Maintenance of International Peace and Security." *International Organization* 19 (3): 429–33.

Gordon, Michael R., and Bernard E. Trainor. 2006. *Cobra II: The Inside Story of the Invasion and Occupation of Iraq*. New York: Pantheon Books.

Gordon, Philip H., and Jeremy Shapiro. 2004. *Allies at War: Europe, America, and the Crisis over Iraq*. New York: McGraw-Hill.

Grant, Ruth W., and Robert O. Keohane. 2005. "Accountability and Abuses of Power in World Politics." *American Political Science Review* 99 (1): 29–44.

Grieco, Joseph. 2003. "Let's Get a Second Opinion: Allies, the UN, and U.S. Public Support for War." Unpublished manuscript, Duke University.

Grief, Avner. 1998. "Self-Enforcing Political Systems and Economic Growth: Late Medieval Genoa." In *Analytic Narratives*, ed. Robert Bates, Avner Grief, Margaret Levi, Jean-Laurent Rosenthal, and Barry R. Weingast, 23–63. Princeton, NJ: Princeton University Press.

Guisinger, Alexandra, and Alastair Smith. 2002. "Honest Threats." *Journal of Conflict Resolution* 46 (2): 175–200.

Guzman, Andrew T. 2008. *How International Law Works: A Rational Choice Theory*. New York: Oxford University Press.

Haas, Ernst B. 1990. *When Knowledge Is Power*. Berkeley, CA: University of California Press.

Hafner-Burton, Emilie, and Kiyo Tsutsui. 2005. "Human Rights Practice in a Globalizing World: The Paradox of Empty Promises." *American Journal of Sociology* 110 (5): 1373–411.

Haftel, Yoram. 2007. "Designing for Peace: Regional Integration Arrangements, Institutional Variation, and Militarized Interstate Disputes." *International Organization* 61 (1): 217–37.

Halberstam, David. 2001. *War in a Time of Peace: Bush, Clinton, and the Generals*. New York: Simon & Schuster.

Havilend, H. Field. 1965. "The United States and the United Nations." *International Organization* 19 (3): 643–55.

Heckman, James J. 1979. "Sample Selection Bias as a Specification Error." *Econometrica* 47 (1): 153–62.

Hodges, Tony. 1983. *Western Sahara: Roots of a Desert War*. Westport, CT: Lawrence Hill.

Holsti, Ole. 1996. *Public Opinion and American Foreign Policy*. Ann Arbor: University of Michigan Press.

Hopf, Theodore J. 1994. *Peripheral Visions: Deterrence Theory and American Foreign Policy*. Ann Arbor: University of Michigan Press.

Hurd, Ian. 1999. "Legitimacy and Authority in International Politics." *International Organization* 53 (2): 397–408.

————. 2002. "Legitimacy, Power, and the Symbolic Life of the UN Security Council." *Global Governance* 8: 35–51.

————. 2007. *After Anarchy: Legitimacy and Authority in the United Nations Security Council.* Princeton, NJ: Princeton University Press.

Huth, Paul, and Todd Allee. 2006. "Legitimizing Dispute Settlement: International Rulings as Domestic Political Cover." *American Political Science Review* 100 (2): 219–34.

Ikenberry, G. John. 2001. *After Victory: Institutions, Strategic Restraint, and the Rebuilding of Order after Major Wars.* Princeton, NJ: Princeton University Press.

Jentleson, Bruce. 1992. "The Pretty Prudent Public: Post Post-Vietnam American Opinion on the Use of Military Force." *International Studies Quarterly* 36 (March): 49–74.

Jentleson, Bruce, and Rebecca Britton. 1998. "Still Pretty Prudent: Post–Cold War American Public Opinion on the Use of Military Force." *Journal of Conflict Resolution* 42 (August): 395–417.

James, Patrick, and Jean Sebastian Rioux. 1998. "International Crises and Linkage Politics." *Political Research Quarterly* 51: 781–813.

Johnston, Alastair Iain. 2001. "Treating International Institutions as Social Environments." *International Studies Quarterly* 45: 487–516.

————. 2003. "The Social Effects of International Institutions on Domestic (Foreign Policy) Actors." In *Locating the Proper Authorities: The Interaction of Domestic and International Institutions,* ed. Daniel W. Drezner, 145–96. Ann Arbor: University of Michigan Press.

Johnstone, Ian. 2004. "US-UN Relations after Iraq: The End of the World (Order) as We Know It?" *European Journal of International Law* 15 (December): 813–38.

Jones, Daniel M., Stuart A. Bremer, and J. David Singer. 1996. "Militarized Interstate Disputes, 1816–1992: Rationale, Coding Rules, and Empirical Patterns." *Conflict Management and Peace Science* 15: 163–213.

Jupille, Joseph. 2004. *Procedural Politics: Issues, Influence, and Institutional Choice in the European Union.* Cambridge, UK: Cambridge University Press.

Karnow, Stanley. 1983. *Vietnam: A History.* New York: Penguin Books.

Keohane, Robert O. 1984. *After Hegemony: Cooperation and Discord in the World Political Economy.* Princeton, NJ: Princeton University Press.

Keohane, Robert O., Andrew Moravscik, and Anne-Marie Slaughter. 2000. "Legalized Dispute Resolution: Interstate and Transnational." *International Organization* 54 (3): 457–88.

Kinsella, David, and Bruce Russett. 2002. "Conflict Emergence in Interactive Dyads." *Journal of Politics* 64 (4): 1045–68.

Koremenos, Barbara. 2005. "Contracting Around International Uncertainty." *American Political Science Review* 99 (4): 549–66.

Koremenos, Barbara, Charles Lipson, and Duncan Snidal. 2001. "The Rational Design of International Institutions." *International Organization* 55 (4): 761–99.

Kratochwil, Friedrich V., and John Gerard Ruggie. 1986. "International Organization: A State of the Art on an Art of the State." *International Organization* 40: 753–75.

Kull, Steven, and I. M. Destler. 1999. *Misreading the Public: The Myth of a New Isolationism.* Washington, DC: Brookings Institute.

Kydd, Andrew. 2003. "Which Side Are You On? Bias, Credibility and Mediation." *American Journal of Political Science* 47 (4): 597–611.

Lake, David A., and Patrick M. Morgan, eds. 1997. *Regional Orders: Building Security in a New World.* University Park: Pennsylvania State University Press.

Lai, Brian, and Dan Reiter. 2004. "Rally 'Round the Union Jack? Public Opinion and the Use of Force in the United Kingdom, 1948–2001." *International Studies Quarterly* 49: 255–72.

Lee, Jong R. 1977. "Rallying around the Flag: Foreign Policy Events and Presidential Popularity." *Presidential Studies Quarterly* 7 (4): 252–56.

Leeds, Brett Ashley. 2003. "Alliance Reliability in Times of War: Explaining State Decisions to Violate Treaties." *International Organization* 57: 801–27.

Leeds, Brett Ashley, and David R. Davis. 1997. "Domestic Political Vulnerability and International Disputes." *Journal of Conflict Resolution* 41: 814–34.

Leventoglu, Bahar, and Ahmer Tarar. 2005. "Prenegotiation and Public Commitment in Domestic and International Bargaining." *American Political Science Review* 99 (3): 419–33.

Levy, Jack S. 1988. "Domestic Politics and War." *Journal of Interdisciplinary History* 18 (4): 653–73.

———. 1989. "The Diversionary Theory of War: A Critique." In *Handbook of War Studies*, ed. Manus I. Midlarsky, 259–88. London: Unwin-Hyman.

Lian, Bradley, and John R. Oneal. 1993. "Presidents, the Use of Military Force, and Public Opinion." *Journal of Conflict Resolution* 27: 277–300.

Lippman, Walter. 1925. *The Phantom Public.* New York: Macmillan.

Lipson, Charles. 2003. *Reliable Partners: How Democracies Have Made a Separate Peace.* Princeton, NJ: Princeton University Press.

Long, J. S. 1997. *Regression Models for Categorical and Limited Dependent Variables*. Thousand Oaks, CA: Sage Publications.

Lupia, Arthur, and Mathew D. McCubbins. 1998. *The Democratic Dilemma: Can Citizens Learn What They Need to Know?* New York: Cambridge University Press.

MacKuen, Michael B. 1983. "Political Drama, Economic Conditions, and the Dynamics of Presidential Popularity." *American Journal of Political Science* 27: 165–92.

Malone, David M. 1998. *Decision-Making in the UN Security Council: The Case of Haiti, 1990–1997.* Oxford: Clarendon Press.

———, ed. 2004. *The UN Security Council: From the Cold War to the 21st Century.* Boulder, CO: Lynne Rienner.

Malone, David, and Yuen Foong Khong. 2003. "Resisting the Unilateral Impulse." In *Unilateralism and U.S. Foreign Policy*, ed. David Malone and Yuen Foong Khong, 421–30. Boulder, CO: Lynne Rienner.

Mansfield, Edward D., and Helen Milner. 1999. "The New Wave of Regionalism." *International Organization* 53 (3): 589–627.

Mansfield, Edward, Helen V. Milner, and B. Peter Rosendorff. 2002. "Why Democracies Cooperate More: Electoral Control and International Trade Agreements." *International Organization* 56 (3): 477–513.

Mansfield, Edward D., and Jon C. Pevehouse. 2005. "Democratization and International Organizations." *International Organization* 60 (1): 137–67.

Maoz, Zeev, and Bruce Russett. 1993. "Normative and Structural Causes of Democratic Peace, 1946–1986." *American Political Science Review* 87 (3): 640–54.

March, James, and Johan Olsen. 1998. "The Institutional Dynamics of International Political Orders." *International Organization* 52 (4): 943–69.

Marfleet, B. Gregory, and Colleen Miller. 2005. "Failure after 1441: Bush and Chirac in the Security Council." *Foreign Policy Analysis* 1 (3): 249–384.

Martin, Lisa. 1992. *Coercive Cooperation: Explaining Multilateral Economic Sanctions.* Princeton, NJ: Princeton University Press.

Martin, Lisa, and Beth Simmons. 1998. "Theories and Empirical Studies of International Institutions." *International Organization* 52 (4): 943–69.

Mearsheimer, John. 1995. "The False Promise of International Institutions." *International Security* 19 (3): 5–49.

Mercer, Jonathan. 1996. *Reputation and International Politics.* Ithaca, NY: Cornell University Press.

Meernik, James. 2000. "Modeling International Crises and the Political Use of Force by the USA." *Journal of Peace Research* 37 (5): 547–62.

Milgrom, Paul, Douglass C. North, and Barry R. Weingast. 1990. "The Role of Institutions in the Revival of Trade: The Medieval Law Merchant, Private Judges, and the Champagne Fairs." *Economics and Politics* 2 (March): 1–23.

Miller, Ross A. 1995. "Domestic Structures and the Diversionary Use of Force." *American Journal of Political Science* 39 (3): 760–86.

Milner, Helen. 1997. *Interests, Institutions, and Information: Domestic Politics and International Relations*. Princeton, NJ: Princeton University Press.

Mitzen, Jennifer. 2005. "Reading Habermas in Anarchy: Multilateral Diplomacy and Global Public Spheres." *American Political Science Review* 99 (3): 401–17.

Morgan, T. Clifton, and Sally Campbell. 1991. "Domestic Structure, Decisional Constraints, and War: So Why Kant Democracies Fight?" *Journal of Conflict Resolution* 35 (2): 187–211.

Morelli, Massimo, and Giovanni Maggi. 2006. "Self-Enforcing Voting in International Organizations." *American Economic Review* 96 (4): 1137–58.

Mueller, John. 1970. Presidential Popularity from Truman to Johnson. *American Political Science Review* 64 (1): 18–34.

———. 1973. *War, Presidents, and Public Opinion*. Lanham, MD: University Press of America. 64 (1): 18–34.

———. 1994. *Policy and Opinion in the Gulf War*. Chicago: University of Chicago Press.

Nye, Joseph. 2003. "U.S. Power and Strategy after Iraq." *Foreign Affairs* 82 (4): 60–73.

Oneal, John R., Brad Lian, and James H. Joyner. 1996. "Are the American People 'Pretty Prudent?' Public Responses to U.S. Uses of Force, 1950–1988." *International Studies Quarterly* 40 (2): 261–79.

O'Neill, Barry. 1996. "Power and Satisfaction in the United Nations Security Council." *Journal of Conflict Resolution* 40 (2): 219–37.

Oatley, Thomas and Jason Yackee. 2004. "American Interests and IMF Lending." *International Politics* 41 (3): 415–29.

Page, Benjamin I., and Marshall M. Bouton. 2006. *The Foreign Policy Disconnect: What Americans Want from Our Leaders but Don't Get*. Chicago: University of Chicago Press.

Page, Benjamin I., and Robert Y. Shapiro. 1982. "Changes in Americans' Policy Preferences, 1935–1979." *Public Opinion Quarterly* 46 (1): 24–42.

———. 1992. *The Rational Public: Fifty Years of Trends in Americans' Policy Preferences*. Chicago: University of Chicago Press.

Page, Benjamin I., Robert Y. Shapiro, and G.R. Dempsey. 1987. "What Moves Public Opinion?" *American Political Science Review* 81(1): 23–44.

Parker, Suzanne. 1995. "Toward an Understanding of "Rally Effects": Public Opinion in the Persian Gulf War." *Public Opinion Quarterly* 59: 526–46.

Pevehouse, Jon C. 2005. *Democracy from Above? Regional Organizations and Democratization.* New York: Cambridge University Press.

Pevehouse, Jon C., and William G. Howell. 2007. *While Dangers Gather: Congressional Checks on Presidential War Powers.* Princeton, NJ: Princeton University Press.

PIPA (Program on International Policy Attitudes). 2007. "World Publics Favor New Powers for the UN." May 9, 2007. http://www.worldpublic opinion.org.

Prantl, Jochen. 2005. "Informal Groups of States and the UN Security Council." *International Organization* 59 (3): 559–92.

Putnam, Robert. 1988. "Diplomacy and Domestic Politics: The Logic of Two-Level Games." *International Organization* 42 (3): 427–60.

Raymond, Gregory A. 1994. "Democracies, Disputes, and Third Party Intermediaries." *Journal of Conflict Resolution* 38 (1): 24–42.

Reed, William. 2000. "A Unified Model of Conflict Onset and Escalation." *American Journal of Political Science* 44 (1): 84–93.

Reinhardt, Eric. 2001. "Adjudication without Enforcement in GATT Disputes." *Journal of Conflict Resolution* 45 (2): 174–95.

———. 2003. "Tying Hands without a Rope: Rational Domestic Response to International Institutional Constraints." In *Locating the Proper Authorities: The Interaction of Domestic and International Institutions,* ed. Daniel W. Drezner, 77–104. Ann Arbor: University of Michigan Press.

Reiter, Dan, and Curtis Meek. 1999. "Determinants of Military Strategy, 1903–1994: A Quantitative Empirical Test." *International Studies Quarterly* 43: 363–87.

Reiter, Dan, and Allan Stam. 2002. *Democracies at War.* Princeton, NJ: Princeton University Press.

Richards, Diana, T. Clifton Morgan, Rick K. Wilson, Valerie Schweback, and Garry D. Young. 1993. "Good Times, Bad Times, and the Diversionary Use of Force: A Tale of Some Not-So-Free Agents." *Journal of Conflict Resolution* 37: 504–35.

Risse-Kappen, Thomas. 1994. "Ideas Do Not Float Freely: Transnational Coalitions, Domestic Structures, and the End of the Cold War." *International Organization* 48 (2): 185–214.

Rivers, Doug, and N. Rose. 1985. "Passing the President's Program." *American Journal of Political Science* 29 (2): 183–96.

Roberts, Adam. 1995. "From San Francisco to Sarajevo: the UN and the Use of Force." *Survival* 37 (4): 7–28.

————. 1999. "NATO's 'Humanitarian War' Over Kosovo." *Survival* 41 (3): 102–23.

————. 2003. "Law and the Use of Force after Iraq." *Survival* 45 (2): 31–56.

————. 2004. "The Use of Force." In *The UN Security Council*, ed. David M. Malone, 133–52. Boulder, CO: Lynne Rienner.

Rogers, James R. 2001. "Information and Judicial Review: A Signaling Game of Legislative-Judicial Interaction." *American Journal of Political Science* 45 (1): 84–99.

Rohde, David W., and Dennis M. Simon. 1985. "Presidential Vetoes and Congressional Response." *American Journal of Political Science* 29 (3): 397–427.

Rosendorff, B. Peter. 2005. "Stability and Rigidity: Politics and the Design of the WTO's Dispute Settlement Procedure." *American Political Science Review* 99 (3): 389–400.

Rosendorff, B. Peter, and Helen Milner. 2001. "The Optimal Design of International Trade Institutions: Uncertainty and Escape." *International Organization* 55 (4): 829–57.

Rubin, James. 2003. "Stumbling Into War." *Foreign Affairs* (Sept.–Oct.): 46–66.

Russett, Bruce, and Soo Yeon Kim. 1996. "The New Politics of Voting Alignments in the UN General Assembly." *International Organization* 50 (3): 629–52.

Russett, Bruce, and John Oneal. 2001. *Triangulating Peace: Democracy, Interdependence, and International Organizations.* New York: Norton.

Sartori, Anne. 2005. *Deterrence by Diplomacy.* Princeton, NJ: Princeton University Press.

Schacter, Oscar. 1989. "Self-Defense and the Rule of Law." *American Journal of International Law* 83 (2): 259–77.

Schultz, Kenneth. 1999. "Do Democratic Institutions Constrain or Inform? Contrasting Two Institutional Perspectives on Democracy and War. " *International Organization* 52 (2): 233–66.

————. 2001a. *Democracy and Coercive Diplomacy.* Cambridge: Cambridge University Press.

————. 2001b. "Looking for Audience Costs." *Journal of Conflict Resolution* 45 (1): 32–60.

————. 2003. "Tying Hands and Washing Hands: The U.S. Congress and Multilateral Humanitarian Intervention." In *Locating the Proper Authorities: The Interaction of International and Domestic Institutions*, ed. Daniel Drezner, 105–42. Ann Arbor: University of Michigan Press.

————. 2005. "The Politics of Risking Peace: Do Hawks or Doves Extend the Olive Branch?" *International Organization* 59 (1): 1–38.

Sigelman, Lee, and Pamela Johnston Conover. 1981. "The Dynamics of Presidential Support during International Conflict Situations: The Iranian Hostage Crisis." *Political Behavior* 3 (4): 303–18.

Signorino, Curtis A. 1999. Strategic Interaction and the Statistical Analysis of International Conflict. *American Political Science Review* 93 (2): 279–98.

———. 2002. "Strategy and Selection in International Relations." *International Interactions* 28(March): 93–115.

Signorino, Curtis A., and Jeffrey Ritter. 1999. "Tau-b or not Tau-b." *International Studies Quarterly* 43 (1): 115–44.

Signorino, Curtis A., and Ahmer Tarar. 2006. "A Unified Model and Test of Extended Immediate Deterrence." *American Journal of Political Science* 50 (3): 586–605.

Signorino, Curtis A., and Kuzey Yilmaz. 2003. "Strategic Misspecification in Regression Models." *American Journal of Political Science* 47 (3): 551–66.

Simmons, Beth. 2000. "The Legalization of International Monetary Affairs." *International Organization* 54 (3): 573–602.

Slater, Jerome. 1969. "The Limits of Legitimation in International Organizations: The Organization of American States and the Dominican Crisis." *International Organization* 23 (1): 48–72.

Slaughter, Anne-Marie. 2003. "Misreading the Record." *Foreign Affairs* 82 (4): 202–4.

Smith, Alastair. 1996. "Diversionary Foreign Policy in Democratic Systems." *International Studies Quarterly* 40 (1): 133–53.

———. 1998. "International Crises and Domestic Politics." *American Political Science Review* 92 (3): 623–38.

———. 1999. "Testing Theories of Strategic Choice." *American Journal of Political Science* 43 (4): 1254–83.

Stone, Randall. 2004. "The Political Economy of IMF Lending in Africa." *American Political Science Review* 98 (4): 577–93.

Suchman, M. C. 1995. "Managing Legitimacy: Strategic and Institutional Approaches." *Academy of Management Review* 20 (3): 571–610.

Tago, Atsushi. 2005. "Determinants of Multilateralism in US Use of Force: State of Economy, Election Cycle, and Divided Government." *Journal of Peace Research* 42 (5): 585–604.

Tannewald, Nina. 1999. "The Nuclear Taboo: The United States and the Normative Basis of Nuclear Non-Use." *International Organization* 53 (3): 433–68.

Tarar, Ahmer. 2001. "International Bargaining With Two-Sided Domestic Constraints." *Journal of Conflict Resolution* 45 (3): 320–40.

————. 2005. "Constituencies and Preferences in International Bargaining." *Journal of Conflict Resolution* 49 (3): 383–407.

————. 2006. "Diversionary Incentives and the Bargaining Approach to War." *International Studies Quarterly* 50 (1): 169–88.

Thacker, Strom. 1999. "The High Politics of IMF Lending." *World Politics* 52 (1): 38–75.

Tharoor, Sashi. 2003. "Why America Still Needs the United Nations." *Foreign Affairs* 82: 67–80.

Thompson, Alexander. 2006. "Coercion through IOs: The Security Council and the Logic of Information Transmission." *International Organization* 60 (1): 1–3.

————. 2009. *Channeling Power: The UN Security Council and U.S. Statecraft in Iraq.* Ithaca, NY: Cornell University Press.

Tobin, James. 1958. "Estimation of Relationships for Limited Dependent Variables." *Econometrica* 26: 24–36.

Tomz, Michael. 2007a. "The Effect of International Law on Preferences and Beliefs." Working paper, Stanford University.

————. 2007b. "Domestic Audience Costs in International Relations: An Experimental Approach." *International Organization* 61 (4): 821–40.

Tocqueville, Alexis de. 1958. *Democracy in America.* Vol. 1. New York: Vintage.

Tyler, Tom R. 2006. "Psychological Perspectives on Legitimacy and Legitimation." *Annual Review of Psychology* 57: 375–400.

Voeten, Erik. 2000. "Clashes in the Assembly." *International Organization* 54 (2): 185–216.

————. 2001. "Outside Options and the Logic of Security Council Action." *American Political Science Review* 95 (4): 845–59.

————. 2004. "Resisting the Lonely Superpower." *Journal of Politics* 66 (3): 728–54.

————. 2005. "The Political Origins of the UN Security Council's Ability to Legitimize the Use of Force." *International Organization* 59 (3): 527–57.

Vreeland, James R. 2003. *The IMF and Economic Growth.* New York: Cambridge University Press.

Wainstock, Dennis D. 1999. *Truman, MacArthur, and the Korean War.* Westport, CT: Greenwood Press.

Wallensteen, Peter, and Patrik Johanssen. 2004. "Security Council Decisions in Perspective." In *The UN Security Council: From the Cold War to the 21st Century,* ed. David M. Malone, 17–36. Boulder, CO: Lynne Rienner.

Waltz, Kenneth N. 1979. *Theory of International Politics.* New York: McGraw-Hill.

Wedgewood, Ruth. 2003. "The Fall of Saddam Hussein: Security Council Mandates and Preemptive Self-Defense." *The American Journal of International Law* 97 (3): 576–85.

Weingast, Barry R. 1997. "The Political Foundations of Democracy and the Rule of Law." *American Political Science Review* 91 (2): 245–63.

Wendt, Alexander. 1992. "Anarchy Is What States Make of It: The Social Construction of Power Politics." *International Organization* 46 (2): 391–425.

————. 1994. "Collective Identity Formation and the International State." *American Political Science Review* 88 (2): 384–96.

Western, Jon. 2002. "Sources of Humanitarian Intervention: Beliefs, Information, and Advocacy in the U.S. Decisions on Somalia and Bosnia." *International Security* 26 (4): 112–42.

————. 2005. *Selling Intervention: The Presidency, the Media, and the American Public.* Baltimore: Johns Hopkins University Press.

Winter, Eyal. 1996. "Voting and Vetoing." *American Political Science Review* 90 (4): 813–23.

Woodward, Bob. 2004. *Plan of Attack.* New York: Simon & Schuster.

Wolford, Scott. 2007. "The Turnover Trap: New Leaders, Reputation, and International Conflict." *American Journal of Political Science* 51 (4): 772–88.

Zaller, John. 1992. *Nature and Origins of Mass Opinion.* New York: Cambridge University Press.

Zartman, I. William. 1989. *Ripe for Resolution: Conflict and Intervention in Africa.* New York: Oxford University Press.

INDEX

Abbott, Kenneth W., 21, 43, 76
Afghanistan, 30, 106, 111, 113, 119, 123
African Union, 89
aggregate interests, 7, 13, 35, 44, 102, 110, 114, 142
Aldrich, John H., 35
allies, 1–2, 18, 157; coalition building and, 131–39, 142–47; information transmission and, 43, 59; public opinion and, 104–10, 114; security organizations and, 74, 77–78, 82, 84, 89–90; value of multilateral authorization and, 20, 28
Almond, Gabriel, 34
approval: to alleviate action costs, 74; alternative normative explanations and, 79–80; for appearance of non-aggression, 73, 79; audience beliefs and, 101–30; capacity of punishment and, 73; consensus and, 23, 29–30, 35, 43, 59, 74–75, 157–59; contradiction of member states and, 66, 74–75; data analysis of, 116–28; determinants of institutional multilateralism and, 76–79; experimental analysis and, 121–26, 129–30; external public opinion and, 1–4, 9, 16, 18, 36, 73, 75, 119, 131, 161–62 (see also public opinion); forum shopping and, 89–94; to free domestic

constraints, 73–74, 79–80; historical perspective on, 10–13, 19; International Crisis Behavior Project and, 6; international law and, 2, 4n7, 5, 19–20, 23–29, 33, 34n18; legitimacy and, 2, 5–6 (see also legitimacy); presidential ratings and, 56, 107–8, 111, 157; prior level of, 115; rallies and, 110–19; reasons for seeking, 73–100; Resolution 1441 and, 1n1, 109; Resolution 678 and, 106n7; statistical analysis and, 82–85; strategic success and, 73–74; testable predictions and, 80–82; third-party intermediaries and, 79; timing of, 6; toward a strategic theory of, 36; understanding reasons for seeking, 4, 73–100
Arab League, 12, 77, 90, 106, 106n7, 139
Argentina, 3, 104
Aristide, Jean-Bertrand, 2, 13–14
Atlanta Journal-Constitution, 46
audience costs, 63–64
Australia, 3, 78, 132, 139
authorization: alternative normative explanations and, 79–80; consensus and, 23, 29–30, 35, 43, 59, 74–75, 157–59; data analysis of, 116–28; determinants of multilateralism and, 76–79; experimental